Russian Phrase Book

Over 1000 Essential Russian Phrases You Don't Want to Be Without on Your Trip to Russia

© Copyright 2019

All Rights Reserved. No part of this book may be reproduced in any form without permission in writing from the author. Reviewers may quote brief passages in reviews.

Disclaimer: No part of this publication may be reproduced or transmitted in any form or by any means, mechanical or electronic, including photocopying or recording, or by any information storage and retrieval system, or transmitted by email without permission in writing from the publisher.

While all attempts have been made to verify the information provided in this publication, neither the author nor the publisher assumes any responsibility for errors, omissions or contrary interpretations of the subject matter herein.

This book is for entertainment purposes only. The views expressed are those of the author alone, and should not be taken as expert instruction or commands. The reader is responsible for his or her own actions.

Adherence to all applicable laws and regulations, including international, federal, state and local laws governing professional licensing, business practices, advertising and all other aspects of doing business in the US, Canada, UK or any other jurisdiction is the sole responsibility of the purchaser or reader.

Neither the author nor the publisher assumes any responsibility or liability whatsoever on the behalf of the purchaser or reader of these materials. Any perceived slight of any individual or organization is purely unintentional.

Contents

INTRODUCTION 1

CHAPTER 1 2

1.1. THE ALPHABET, READING, AND PRONUNCIATION 2

1.2. BASIC GRAMMAR CONCEPTS 8

CHAPTER 2. NUMERALS 15

2.1. CARDINAL NUMERALS 15

2.2. ORDINAL NUMERALS 20

CHAPTER 3. BASIC NECESSITIES FOR COMMUNICATION 23

3.1. GENERAL EXPRESSIONS AND GREETINGS 23

3.2. LANGUAGE AND MAKING YOURSELF UNDERSTOOD 27

3.3. TALKING ON THE PHONE 29

3.4. DOCUMENTS 30

CHAPTER 4. TALKING ABOUT YOURSELF 32

4.1. INTRODUCING YOURSELF 32

4.2. FAMILY AND RELATIONSHIPS 35

4.3. PROFESSIONS AND OCCUPATIONS 39

4.4. INTERESTS 43

CHAPTER 5. GETTING AROUND 49

5.1. AIRPORT 49

5.2. AROUND THE CITY 58

5.2. TRAINS 64

5.4. PUBLIC TRANSPORT 70

5.5. CARS 74

CHAPTER 6. SIGHTSEEING AND ENTERTAINMENT 80

6.1. SIGHTSEEING 80

6.2. INSIDE A MUSEUM OR THEATER, ETC. 87

CHAPTER 7. SHOPPING AND BANKING 95

7.1. FINANCES 95

7.1. GENERAL SHOPPING 100

7.3. BUYING CLOTHES, SHOES, ACCESSORIES, AND JEWELRY 106

7.4. BUYING BOOKS, PRESS, STATIONERY, SOUVENIRS, AND FLOWERS 113

7.5. BUYING ELECTRONICS AND HOUSEHOLDWARE 117

7.6. BUYING MEDICINE, COSMETICS, AND PERSONAL HYGIENE PRODUCTS 119

CHAPTER 8. ACCOMMODATION, EATING AND SERVICES 122

8.1. HOTELS, HOSTELS AND FLATS 122

8.2. FOOD AND RESTAURANTS 129

8.3. POST, MOBILE AND INTERNET SERVICE 141

CHAPTER 9. HEALTH AND SAFETY 144

9.1. MEDICAL CONDITIONS AND EMERGENCIES 144

9.2. EMERGENCY SITUATIONS 150

CHAPTER 10. TIME AND MEASUREMENTS 153

10.1. MEASUREMENTS 153

10.2. TIME 154

Introduction

We are very glad to introduce you to this brief and effective Russian Phrasebook. Here, you will find 1000+ essential phrases that will help you survive among Russian speaking people, as well as some basic information about reading and pronunciation in Russian, the alphabet, some grammar, and cultural concepts. The Russian language is considered – and very justifiably – to be a very difficult one but it is also very interesting, musical, and beautiful in many ways. So, try the language and do not be afraid to speak it any way you can, do not be afraid of making mistakes. Native Russian speakers are usually quite sympathetic to brave open-minded foreigners who are trying to communicate in their challenging mother tongue. So, go for it, and you will definitely be able to explain yourself if you follow this guide.

Good luck! We hope that you will find this book useful and you will enjoy your first brief encounter with Russian.

Chapter 1

1.1. The Alphabet, Reading, and Pronunciation

If you have ever come across Russian writing, you probably know that the alphabet is quite different if we compare it to the English one. It contains **33** letters. Some of them look like the ones from the Latin alphabet, while some look Greek. Some Russian letters are unique, and some can be quite misleading – e.g. the letter "Н н" looks like the English H h but sounds like [n].

The letters look a bit exotic, but the good news is – they are very easy to read. If we compare English and Russian, the reading rules in the latter are rather simple; usually, the letters are directly connected to the sounds they represent without any tricky vowel and consonant combinations. Surely, there are some spelling rules and exceptions, but reading is much easier to master than in English.

Here, we will introduce the letters themselves as well as the sounds they represent. Therefore, after some practicing, you will be able to read texts in Russian as well as pronounce the words.

Surely, you have heard Russians speaking English – if only in movies – and have some idea of how a Russian accent sounds. It has some particular features that are the result of the pronunciation of the Russian language. Of course, it works the other way around – English speakers pronounce Russian words with a strong accent as well. Thus, we will start with some typical aspects of the Russian accent and pronunciation because it will help you minimize your *own* foreign accent when speaking Russian, and better understand Russian speech.

In general, Russian sounds are less clearly articulated than the English ones, e.g. Russian speakers move their lips in a much more relaxed way when speaking, and they pronounce sounds less prominently. You can see it if you pay attention while communicating with your Russian counterparts.

There is one pronunciation trend that is connected with this relaxed articulation – voiced consonants typically become silent at the end of Russian words. Say, you have two words плод – fruit – and плот – raft – the consonants at the end are different here – д [d] and т [t], but the words sound absolutely the same [plɒt], as the voiced д [d] turns into the unvoiced т [t]. Surely, we will use phonetic symbols for the phrases listed in the book, but please keep this feature in mind when reading and pronouncing Russian words.

There are some unique Russian sounds that will need special training – e.g. a vowel ы or consonants ц and щ – we will point them out further on. Nevertheless, many sounds are similar to English ones although the letters representing them may seem different.

There are ten vowel letters in Russian but only six vowel sounds – [а], [о], [у] [э] [и] [ы]. There are no diphthongs or distinguishable long and short vowels.

There are 21 consonant letters in Russian but 37 consonant sounds. The reason for this difference is the ability of some consonants to become palatalized or softened. As a result, there are many consonant pairs which are considered to be two different sounds. This is a very important aspect of Russian pronunciation as there is no palatalization in English, where all consonants are always hard. A consonant being hard or soft can totally change the meaning – e.g. мол [mɒl] – jetty and моль [mɒl'] – moth. Note that we are going to use an apostrophe (') symbol to mark soft consonants.

To make a consonant soft you should – while pronouncing it – slightly raise the middle part of your tongue to your hard palate.

Unfortunately, there are no regular stress patterns for Russian words and any syllable can be emphasized. So – the only advice here is to check. Here, of course, we will mark the stress for all the words with the symbol ˋ. Please pay attention to it as stress is very important and it also can totally change the meaning – e.g. ˋз<u>а</u>мок [ˋzʌmɒk] – castle and за<u>ˋмок</u> [zʌˋmɒk] – lock.

Now, we will go through the alphabet and the basic pronunciation characteristics as the letters are directly connected with the sounds. Here, and further on, we will use standard phonetic symbols for you to be able to decipher the words.

А а [ʌ] – is the first letter and the first vowel sound. As there are no long / short vowels in Russian, this sound is always short. It sounds a lot like [ʌ] in "cut". Here are some words with it - ˋм<u>ама</u> [ˋmʌmʌ] – mum, ˋп<u>апа</u> [ˋpʌpʌ] – dad, <u>ал</u>ˋло [ʌˋlɒ] – a telephone greeting.

Б б [be] – the letter reads as a consonant similar to [b] in "big" – e.g. ˋ<u>бабу</u>шка [ˋbʌbʊʃkʌ] – grandma / an old lady. Б can be softened – compare <u>бы</u>л [byl] – was – <u>би</u>л [b'il] – <he> beat.

В в [ve] – this misleading letter looks like an English capital "B" but it reads as [v] in "vase" – e.g. ˋ<u>буква</u> [ˋbʊkvʌ]. В also can be softened – compare <u>во</u>л [vɒl] – ox – <u>вё</u>л [v'ɒl] – <he> led.

Г г [ge] – this consonant reads like [g] in "give" – e.g. ти<u>гр</u> [tigr] – tiger. Г also can be softened.

Д д [de] – this consonant reads a bit like [d] in "dig" but there is an important difference – all the consonants that are alveolar in English are dental in Russian. It means that they are pronounced with the tip of your tongue pressed to your upper teeth rather than to the alveolar ridge – e.g. да [dʌ] – yes. Д also can be softened – compare да-да [dʌ dʌ] yes-yes and `дядя [`d'ʌd'ʌ] – uncle.

Е е [je] – is the second vowel letter. The pronunciation here depends on its position – after consonants, it reads like [e] in "get". This letter usually makes the preceding consonant soft – e.g. `дети [`d'etɪ] – children, `лето [`l'etʌ] – summer. If it is used after a vowel or in the beginning of a word, it reads as [je] sound combination – e.g. `поезд [`pɒjezd] – a train.

Ё ё [jɒ] – is a vowel letter, which is often changed into Е е in printed texts except books for children and language learning. It reads like [ɒ] in "not" after consonants and, like the previous vowel Е е, it makes the preceding consonant soft – e.g. клён [kl'ɒn] – maple, лён [l'ɒn] – linen. Also, after a vowel or at the beginning of a word, it reads as [jɒ] sound combination – e.g. `ёлка [`jɒlkʌ] – Christmas tree. This vowel is *always* stressed.

Ж ж [ʒe] – this consonant reads like [ʒ] in "pleasure" – e.g. жить [ʒit'] – to live, нож [nɒʒ] – knife. This consonant can be only hard – it is *never* softened.

З з [ze] – this consonant reads like [z] in "zoo" – e.g. `завтра [`zʌvtrʌ] – tomorrow. З can be softened.

И и [i] – this vowel reads like [i] in "hit" – e.g. при`вет [`pr'iv'et] – hello. This letter *always* makes the preceding consonant soft.

Й й [j] – this is a consonant or so-called semivowel. It reads like [j] in "yellow" but it is a bit harsher and more prominent in Russian than in English – e.g. да**й** [dʌj] – given in the imperative form. As it is already soft, there is no soft / hard pair for it.

К к [kʌ] – this consonant reads like [k] in "keep", but unlike English, it has no aspiration i.e. forceful expulsion of air – e.g. **к**а**к** [kʌk] – how. This consonant can be softened.

Л л [el] – this consonant reads like [l] in "lot" but it is dental rather than alveolar i.e. pronounced with the tongue pressed to the upper teeth rather than alveoli – `**л**адно ['lʌdnʌ] – OK / agreed. This consonant can be softened.

М м [em] – this consonant like [m] in "mother" – e.g. `**м**оре [`mɒr'e] – sea. This consonant can be softened.

Н н [en] – this consonant reads like [n] in "need" and it is also dental and pronounced with your tongue pressed to the upper teeth – **н**ет [n'et] – no. This consonant can be softened.

О о [ɒ] – this vowel reads like [ɒ] in "got" – e.g. `**о**зер**о** [`ɒz'erʌ] – lake. Note that this letter turns into [ʌ] in an unstressed position as you can see from the example above.

П п [pe] – this consonant reads like [p] in "put". Like [k], it is pronounced without English aspiration – **п**ол [pɒl] – floor. This consonant can be softened.

Р р [er] – this consonant slightly resembles [r] in "right" but with some differences in pronunciation – the tongue should go almost at the alveoli and slightly vibrate; as a result, it sounds a bit like the harsh [r] sound in a Scottish accent – e.g. **р**у`ка [`rʊkʌ] – hand. This consonant can be softened.

С с [es] – this consonant reads almost like [s] in "sit" – e.g. **с**па`**с**ибо [`spʌs'ibʌ] – thank you. This consonant can be softened.

Т т [te] – this consonant reads like [t] in "time" but it is also alveolar – so your tongue must go to your upper teeth rather than alveoli, plus it has no aspiration – e.g. **три** [tr′ɪ] – three. This consonant can be softened.

У у [ʋ] – this vowel reads almost like [ʋ] in "put" – e.g. `**утро** [`ʋtrʌ] – morning.

Ф ф [fe] – this consonant reads like [f] in "fit" – e.g. **фа`милия** [fʌ`m′il′ijʌ] – surname. This consonant can be softened.

Х х [he] – the consonant reads like [h] in "hot" but it is pronounced more harshly and enthusiastically than the English one – e.g. `**плохо** [`plɒhʌ] – bad. This consonant can be softened.

Ц ц [tse] – this unique consonant has no alternatives in English. It resembles the [ts] combination in "its" but it is one sound rather than two separate sounds combined, so you have to pronounce it as one sound – e.g. **це`на** [tse`nʌ] – price. Note that this consonant can only be hard – it is never softened.

Ч ч [tʃe] – this consonant reads like [tʃ] in "chick" but it is always soft – so there is no hard / soft pair – and has less [t] in it than the English [tʃ] – **чело`век** [tʃelʌ`vek] – parson.

Ш ш [ʃe] – this consonant reads like [ʃ] in "shot" – **ш`кола** [`ʃkɒlʌ] – school. This consonant can be only hard – it is never softened.

Щ щ [ʃ′ʌ] – this consonant is tricky – it resembles the previous one [ш] or [ʃ] with one important difference – it is always soft – e.g. `**щетка** [`ʃ′etkʌ] – brush.

ъ – **твёрдый знак** or [`tv′ɒrdyj znʌk] – this letter does not refer to any particular sound – it marks hard consonants – i.e. in the word **о`бъезд** [ʌb`jezd] – alternative route – it makes the letter **б** stay hard even before the letter **е**.

ы [y] – this vowel, which is never used at the beginning of a word, is unique to Russian and somewhat difficult to pronounce. To do it, you should open your mouth in the same way you do it for [i] but your tongue must lay flat – e.g. мы [my] – we.

ь – мягкий знак or [`m'ʌhkij znʌk] – this letter, much like ъ, is not connected to any sound. It usually – but not always – marks the softening of the preceding consonant – e.g. соль [sɒl'] – salt.

Э э [e] – this vowel reads like [e] in "end" – e.g. `Это [`etɒ] – this.

Ю ю [jʊ] – this vowel reads like [ʊ] in "June" after consonants, and at the same time makes the consonants soft – e.g. люк [l'ʊk] – hatch. If this vowel is preceded by another vowel or it goes at the beginning of a word, it reads like [jʊ] in "suit" – e.g. юг [jʊg] – south.

Я я [jʌ] – the reading of this vowel also depends on the preceding letter. After consonants, it reads like [ʌ] in "but" and makes the consonant soft – e.g. `дядя [`d'ʌd'ʌ]. After a vowel or in the beginning of a word, it reads like [jʌ] – e.g. я [`jʌ] – I.

Now you know how to read Russian letters and pronounce Russian sounds. Using this part as your guide, you will be able to decipher Russian texts and recognize Russian sounds.

1.2. Basic Grammar Concepts

Russian grammar is considered – and justifiably – to be quite tough. Of course, we are not going to introduce it in this book, but we will point out some basic grammar concepts for you to grasp the essential differences and know what to expect and where to look, while going through the words and expressions given here.

To start with, Russian and English have different language systems – Russian is a synthetic language and English is primarily an analytic language. It means that English grammar uses word order and some special words – e.g. particles, auxiliary verbs, etc. – to express essential concepts. On the other hand, Russian generally uses inflexions or word endings to express grammar and syntactic relationships e.g. singular and plural forms of the verbs, nouns, pronouns, and even adjectives are expressed with some particular endings.

Then, unlike English, Russian does not have any fixed word order. Surely, there are some sentence patterns, but the words can be easily reorganized. It may change the emphasis or style of a sentence but not the basic meaning. Let's look at this sentence – **На сто`ле ле`жит `книга** [nʌ stɒ`l'e l'e`zit k'nigʌ] – **Книга лежит на столе** [k'nigʌ l'e`zit nʌ stɒ`l'e] – **Лежит книга на столе** [l'e l'e`zit k'nigʌ nʌ stɒ`] – **Книга на столе лежит** [k'nigʌ nʌ stɒ`l'e l'e`zit], etc. These are variations of the same phrase – *There is a book on the table*. Changing word order, we change the stylistic aspects and the focus, but all four variations are grammatically and syntactically correct and represent normal and meaningful speech. Thus, do not be surprised to hear the words from the same phrase combined differently and do not be afraid to change word order – it is not as strict as in English.

If we look at Russian verbs, we will see that they have so called **conjugation** – various forms expressing various grammar meanings – e.g. singular / plural, first / second / third person etc. Let's take as an example the verb `видеть [`vʼidʼetʼ] – "to see" in the Present Tense – `вижу [`vʼiʒʊ] – <I> see, `видишь [`vʼidʼiʃ] – <you – singular> see, `видит [`vʼidʼit] – <he/she/it> sees, `видим [`vʼidʼim] – <we> see, `видите [`vʼidʼitʼe] – <you – plural> see. Because of conjugating, we sometimes do not even need to use any pronouns – one can just say `вижу – and the verb ending will make it clear that a person is talking about him / herself – the first person singular. If we take the same verb in the Past Tense, we will have `видел [`vʼidʼel] <someone of masculine gender> saw, `видела [`vʼidʼelʌ] – <she> saw, `видели [`vʼidʼelʼi] <someone – plural> saw – so here the endings express not only plural/singular aspect but the **gender** as well.

Gender aspect is also very important, when talking about nouns and adjectives. All nouns in Russian have particular genders. There are **masculine, feminine**, and **neuter** gender nouns. Gender aspect is obvious and logical, when we are dealing with people – e.g. `женщина [`ʒenʃʼinʌ] – woman and `мама [`mʌmʌ] – mom are feminine, while `мужчина [`mʊʃʼinʌ] – man and папа [`pʌpʌ] dad are masculine. Nevertheless, not only nouns referring to people but all the nouns in general – animated or unanimated – have a gender, e.g. теле`фон [tʼelʼe`fɒn] – telephone is masculine, `чашка [`tʃlʌʃkʌ] – cup is feminine, and ме`ню [mʼe`nʼʊ] – menu is neuter. Here you just have to know the gender, as it cannot be simply deduced based on the meaning. There are some typical gender endings that may sometimes help you, but they can also be misleading.

Gender is also expressed in adjective endings and in the endings of some pronouns –e.g. the adjective хо`роший [hʌ`rɒʃij] – good, will have three different nominative forms for the three genders – e.g. `эт<u>а</u> хо`рош<u>ая</u> `мама [`etʌ hʌ`rɒʃʌjʌ `mʌmʌ] – this good mom, `Это<u>т</u> хороший папа [`etɒt hʌ`rɒʃij `pʌpʌ] – this good dad, `Это хорош<u>ее</u> меню [`etɒ hʌ`rɒʃeje m'e`n'ʊ] – this good menu.

Thus, as you can see, gender aspect is an extremely important category and it is expressed in nouns, adjectives, and pronouns, as well as in some verb forms. We will provide gender options for some phrases in this book – so sometimes you will see a gender mark – (masculine) or (feminine).

Now, let's discuss personal pronouns, which is a very useful category to know. There are: **я** [jʌ] – I – the first person singular; **ты** [ty] – you – the second person singular; **он** [ɒn] – he, **о`на** [ʌ`nʌ] – she, **о`но** [ʌ`nɒ] – it – the third person singular, which can substitute various nouns depending on the gender; **мы** [my] – we – the first person plural; **вы** [vy] – you – the second person plural, **они** [ʌ`n'i] – they – the third person plural. Here, we are dealing only with nominative grammatical case, which begs the next question – what is a grammatical case?

As you remember, Russian is a synthetic language and grammatical and syntactical meanings are expressed with various endings. Grammatical case is a particular set of forms that nouns, pronouns, adjectives, and numerals can have. These forms – together with prepositions and word order – help to express those various meanings. Moreover, nouns and adjectives of different gender will change differently when various grammatical cases are involved.

To demonstrate it, we will take the phrase **мой `лучший друг** [mɒi `lʊtʃʃij drʊk] – my best friend (masculine) – and use it in various combinations. Please pay attention to the endings here – **`Это м<u>ой</u> `лучш<u>ий</u> друг** [`etʌ mɒi `lʊtʃʃij drʊk] – This is my best friend; **Я гово`рю «при`вет» мое`<u>му</u> `лучш<u>ему</u> `друг<u>у</u>** [jʌ gʌvʌ`r'ʊ pr'i`v'et maje`mʊ `lʊtʃʃemʊ `drʊgʊ] – I say "hello" to my best friend; **Я гово`рю с мо`<u>им</u> `лучш<u>им</u> `друг<u>ом</u>** [jʌ gʌvʌ`r'ʊ s ma`im `lʊtʃʃim `drʊgʌm] – I am talking to my best friend; **Я люб`лю мое`<u>го</u> `лучш<u>его</u> `друг<u>а</u>** [jʌ `l'ʊbl'ʊ mʌje`vɒ `lʊtʃʃevʌ `drʊgʌ] – I love my best friend. You can see that the same pronoun, adjective, and noun change in these sentences depending on the position and meaning because they are used in different grammatical cases.

In total, there are six grammatical cases – nominative, genitive, dative, accusative, instrumental, and prepositional. There are particular meanings, phrases, and prepositions associated with every grammatical case. Every pronoun has special forms for every grammatical case, and some of these forms might differ from the first nominative form – e.g. the personal pronoun **я** [jʌ] – I – will have: **ме`ня** [m'e`n'ʌ], **мне** [mn'e], **ме`ня**, **мной** [mnɒj], and **мне** as its respective grammatical case forms. There are also different endings for nouns, adjectives, and pronouns of various genders in various grammatical cases for singular and plural nouns.

We will not analyze these endings and grammar structures here, but we will, of course, use them – so, do not be confused when in some cases you will see the same words used with different endings in different phrases. Surely, it will not be an irrevocable mistake if you just say a word in its first – nominative – form, or mix up the grammatical cases – you will most likely be able to explain yourself anyway, but using the correct grammatical case will make your speech more comprehensible and elegant.

We will discuss one more important thing that is connected with grammar – i.e. honorific forms.

There are *two* different ways of addressing in Russian. The first way is an informal one, when talking to a friend, a relative, a peer, a person you know well or communicate with in an informal situation. The second way is a formal and polite one, when talking to an older person, a person you have just recently met, or someone you are in formal relationships with. Depending on the situation, you should use two different second person *you*-pronouns – the informal **ты** [ty] and the formal **вы** [vy] – as well as their grammatical case forms and possessive derivatives. Informal **ты** is used for the second person, while **вы** can be used for a) the second person plural, when addressing several people and b) the second person singular – when addressing one person in a formal or polite way. Sometimes, shifting from the formal **вы** to informal **ты** may be a great deal, when communicating with someone. When people do not know each other well or prefer to keep some distance, they use **вы** forms. When their relationships have become closer, they may discuss the matter and decide that they mutually agree to use **ты** with each other now or they may do it intuitively. We recommend using the informal option **вы,** when you are not sure of the nature of your relationships – just to be on the safe side.

Honorifics are also expressed in verb endings for various conjugations. First of all, it concerns the indicative mood – e.g. you can ask someone `**Хоч**е**шь есть?** [`hɒtʃeʃ jest'] or `**Хот**и**те есть?** [`hɒt'it'e jest'] – "Do you want to eat?" The former question is for a singular second person addressed in an informal way; while the latter question can be used for a plural second person as well as for singular second person addressed in a formal and polite way. Then, these two ways of addressing can be expressed also in the imperative mood. There is an ending – **те** [t'e] that is used for the plural form as well as for the singular formal or polite form – e.g. **ешь** [jeʃ] – `**ешь**те [`jeʃt'e] – eat, in the imperative mood – the former addresses one person in an informal way, while the latter addresses several people or one person in a formal polite way.

In this book, we will provide both options when applicable and mark them: (polite) or (informal). So, please pay attention to it when assessing the communication situation.

We will not make things too complicated for you by including any other grammatical structures here, but the ones mentioned above are quite essential – so it will be great if you keep them in mind, while going through this book.

Chapter 2. Numerals

Here we will list Russian numerals for you to use and point out some grammatical nuances connected with them that you will need further on.

2.1. Cardinal Numerals

1 – о`дин [ʌ`d'in]

This particular numeral can have various gender forms depending on a noun it refers to. **О`дин** [ʌ`d'in] is masculine, while for feminine you will need **од`на** [ʌd`nʌ] and for neuter – **од`но** [ʌd`nɒ]. So, do not be surprised to see these different forms in the phrases.

2 – два [dvʌ]

This one also has a separate feminine form **две** [dv'e]

3 – три [tr'i]

4 – че`тыре [tʃe`tyr'e]

5 – пять [p'ʌt']

6 – шесть [ʃest']

7 – семь [s'em']

8 – `восемь [`vɒs'em']

9 – `девять [`d'ev'ʌt']

10 – `десять [`d'es'ʌt']

11 – о`диннадцать [ʌ`d'inʌtsʌt']

12 – две`надцать [dv'e`nʌtsʌt']

13 – три`надцать [tr'i`nʌtsʌt']

14 – че`тырнадцать [tʃe`tyrnʌtsʌt']

15 – пят`надцать [p'ʌt`nʌtsʌt']

16 – шест`надцать [ʃest`nʌtsʌt']

17 – сем`надцать [s'em`nʌtsʌt']

18 – **восем`надцать** [vʌsʼemˋnʌtsʌtʼ]

19 – **девят`надцать** [dʼevʼʌtˋnʌtsʌtʼ]

20 – **`двадцать** [dˋvʌtsʌtʼ]

30 – **`тридцать** [tˋrʼitsʌtʼ]

40 – **`сорок** [ˋsɒrʌk]

50 – **пятьде`сят** [pʼʌtʼeˋsʼʌt]

60 – **шестьде`сят** [ʃestʼeˋsʼʌt]

70 – **`семьдесят** [ˋsemʼdʼesʼʌt]

80 – **`восемьдесят** [ˋvɒsʼemdʼeˋsʼʌt]

90 – **девя`носто** [dʼevʼʌˋnɒstʌ]

You can easily make compound numbers combining the numerals, for example:

22 – **`двадцать два** [dˋvʌtsʌtʼ dvʌ]

35 – **`тридцать пять** [tˋrʼitsʌtʼ pʼʌtʼ]

68 – **шестьде`сят `восемь** [ʃestʼeˋsʼʌt ˋvɒsʼemʼ]

89 – **`восемьдесят `девять** [ˋvɒsʼemdʼeˋsʼʌt ˋdʼevʼʌtʼ] etc.

100 – **сто** [stɒ]

200 – **`двести** [dˋvʼesti]

300 – **`триста** [ˋtristʌ]

400 – **че`тыреста** [tʃeˋtyrʼestʌ]

500 – **пять`сот** [pʼʌtˋsɒt]

600 – **шесть`сот** [ʃesˋsɒt]

700 – **семь`сот** [sʼemˋsɒt]

800 – **восемь`сот** [vʌsʼemˋsɒt]

900 – **девять`сот** [dʼevʼʌtˋsɒt]

Numbers in the hundreds are also easily combined with other numerals to produce compound numbers:

104 – сто че`тыре [stɒ tʃe`tyrʹe]

317 – `триста сем`надцать [`tristʌ sʹem`nʌtsʌtʹ]

438 – че`тыреста `тридцать `восемь [tʃe`tyrʹestʌ t`rʹitsʌtʹ `vɒsʹemʹ]

999 – девять`сот девя`носто `девять [dʹevʹʌt`sɒt dʹevʹʌ`nɒstʌ `dʹevʹʌtʹ]

There is an important grammatical issue that is connected with numerals and nouns in Russian. Unlike English, where you have only one possible plural form for any noun – e.g. dogs, two dogs, many dogs, etc – Russian has different plural forms for nouns depending on the numeral they follow. Here, we will have to remember about Russian grammatical cases mentioned in the previous chapter, as different cases will be used for nouns after different numerals.

Rather than looking into the grammar structure or analyzing grammatical case forms here, we will use a simple formula further on in this book:

> – Nouns after any numeral ending with **1 – except 11**
>
> – Nouns after any numeral ending with **2, 3, 4 – except 12, 13, 14**
>
> – Nouns after the numerals **11-14** or any numeral ending with **0, 5, 6, 7, 8, 9**

Every one of these three options requires a noun in a particular grammatical case after it. Thus, if we need a phrase with a numeral plus a noun combination, we will use this formula to determine which plural grammatical case to use out of the three possible forms for such a noun.

You will also need this grammatical trick for the next bunch of numerals, because those numerals will work just as nouns here. Depending on the number of thousands, millions, billions, etc. the word itself will be used in different grammatical cases according to the formula:

1000 – `тысяча [`tys'ʌtʃʌ]

    – After any numeral ending with **1 – except 11**

21000 – `двадцать од`на `тысяча [d`vʌtsʌt' `ʌdnʌ `tys'ʌtʃʌ]

    – After any numeral ending with **2, 3, 4 – except 12, 13, 14**

2000 – две `тысячи [d`v'e `tys'ʌtʃi]

34 000 – `тридцать че`тыре `тысячи [t`r'itsʌt' tʃe`tyr'e `tys'ʌtʃi]

    – After the numerals **11-14** or any numeral ending with **0, 5, 6, 7, 8, 9**

20 000 – `двадцать `тысяч [d`vʌtsʌt' `tys'ʌtʃ]

14 000 – че`тырнадцать `тысяч [tʃe`tyrnʌtsʌt'`tys'ʌtʃ]

1000 000 – милли`он [m'il'i`ɒn]

    – After any numeral ending with **1 – except 11**

41 000 000 – `сорок од`ин `миллион [`sɒrʌk `ʌdin m'il'i`ɒn]

    – After any numeral ending with **2, 3, 4 – except 12, 13, 14**

3 000 000 – три милли`она [tr'i m'il'i`ɒnʌ]

33 000 0000 – `тридцать три милли`она [t`r'itsʌt' tr'i m'il'i`ɒnʌ]

    – After the numerals **11-14** or any numeral ending with **0, 5, 6, 7, 8, 9**

30 000 000 – `тридцать милли`онов [t`r'itsʌt' m'il'i`ɒnʌf]

15 000 000 - пят`надцать милли`он<u>ов</u> [p'ʌt`nʌtsʌt' m'il'i`ɒnʌf]

1000 000 000 - милли`ард [m'il'i`ʌrd]

- After any numeral ending with **1 – except 11**

51 000 000 000 пятьде`сят о`дин милли`ард [pʌt'e`s'ʌt ʌ`d'in m'il'i`ʌrd]

- After any numeral ending with **2, 3, 4 – except 12, 13, 14**

4 000 000 000 - че`тыре милли`ард<u>а</u> [tʃe`tyr'e m'il'i`ʌrdʌ]

- After the numerals **11-14** or any numeral ending with **0, 5, 6, 7, 8, 9**

11 000 000 000 - о`диннадцать милли`ард<u>ов</u> [ʌ`d'inʌtsʌt' m'il'i`ʌrdʌf]

As you can see, you can use this formula for any numeral combination – you just have to put the word in the correct form. It will work the same way with nouns further on in the book.

One more important thing – please note that you must not use commas for compound numbers in Russian. You should be very careful because commas – rather than dots – are used to mark decimals. Thus, there may be some confusion, if you use compound numbers without proper consideration – e.g. 30,000 in Russian is going to be perceived the same way that 30.000 is perceived in English.

2.2. Ordinal Numerals

The situation with ordinal numerals is a little bit more complicated. They have the same form as adjectives and thus there are multiple endings involved – for plural / singular forms as well as for the three different genders and corresponding grammatical cases, which we discussed in Chapter 1. If we take, say, the ordinal numeral `первый [`p'ervyj] or "first", it, depending on the following noun, will have the following forms only for nominative – `перв**ый** [`p'ervyj] – masculine gender singular e.g. `перв**ый** му`жчина [`p'ervyj mʊ`ʃ'inʌ] – the first man; `перв**ая** [`p'ervʌjʌ] feminine gender singular – e.g. `перв**ая** `женщина [`p'ervʌjʌ `ʒenʃ'inʌ] – the first woman; `перв**ое** [`p'ervʌje] neuter gender singular – e.g. `перв**ое** п`равило [`p'ervʌje p`rʌv'ilʌ] – the first rule; plus `перв**ые** [`p'ervyje] form for nominative plural – e.g. `перв**ые** `люди [`p'ervyje `l'ʊd'i] – the first people; on the top of different endings for each of the five remaining grammatical cases. We will not analyze all the various possible grammar forms here as it will complicate things too much, yet we will list nominative singular masculine forms for reference, as well as provide appropriate grammar forms for the phrases further on in the book.

1st – `первый [`p'ervyj]

2nd – вто`рой [vtʌ`rɒj]

3rd – т`ретий [t`r'et'ij]

4th – чет`вёртый [tʃet`v'ɒrtyj]

5th – `пятый [`p'ʌtyj]

6th – шес`той [ʃes`tɒj]

7th – седь`мой [s'ed'`mɒj]

8th – вось`мой [vʌs'`mɒj]

9th – де`вятый [d'e`v'ʌtyj]

10th – де`сятый [dʲeˋsʌtyj]

11th – о`диннадцатый [ʌˋdʲinʌtsʌtyj]

12th – две`надцатый [dvʲeˋnʌtsʌtyj]

13th – три`надцатый [trʲiˋnʌtsʌtyj]

14th – че`тырнадцатый [tʃeˋtyrnʌtsʌtyj]

15th – пят`надцатый [pʲʌtˋnʌtsʌtyj]

16th – шест`надцатый [ʃestˋnʌtsʌtyj]

17th – сем`надцатый [sʲemˋnʌtsʌtyj]

18th – восем`надцатый [vʌsʲemˋnʌtsʌtyj]

19th – девят`надцатый [dʲevʲʌtˋnʌtsʌtyj]

20th – двад`цатый [dvʌˋtsʌtyj]

30th – трид`цатый [trʲiˋtsʌtyj]

40th – сороко`вой [sʌrʌkʌˋvɒj]

50th – пятиде`сятый [pʲʌtʲidʲeˋsʌtyj]

60th – шестиде`сятый [ʃestʲ idʲeˋsʌtyj]

70th – семиде`сятый [sʲemʲi dʲeˋsʌtyj]

80th – восьмиде`сятый [vʌsʲmiˋdʲeˋsʌtyj]

90th – девя`ностый [dʲevʲʌˋnɒstyj]

Mercifully, if you want to make a compound number, only the last element will be an ordinal numeral, while all the rest will be cardinals:

21st – `двадцать `первый [dˋvʌtsʌtʲ ˋpʲervyj]

36th – `тридцать шес`той [tˋrʲitsʌtʲ ʃesˋtɒj]

222nd – `двести `двадцать вто`рой [dˋvʲesti dˋvʌtsʌtʲ vtʌˋrɒj]

Etc.

100th – `сотый [ˋsɒtyj]

1000th – `**тысячный** [`tys'ʌtʃnyj]

2000th – **двух`тысячный** [dvʊh`tys'ʌtʃnyj]

Now, you have some idea of cardinal and ordinal numerals in Russian, and you can use the numerals above as a reference to make phrases and sentences you need. Now, we will move further on to actual Russian phrases.

Chapter 3. Basic Necessities for Communication

3.1. General Expressions and Greetings

1. Yes – Да [dʌ]

2. No – Нет [n'et]

3. Thank you – Спа`сибо [spʌ`s'ibʌ]

4. Thank you very much – Боль`шое спа`сибо [bʌl'`ʃɒje spʌ`s'ibʌ]

5. Thanks for the information – Спа`сибо за инфор`мацию [spʌ`s'ibʌ zʌ infʌr`mʌtsijʊ]

6. Please – По`жалуйста [pʌ`ʒʌlʊstʌ]

7. You are welcome – `Не за что [`n'ezʌʃtʌ]

8. Excuse me – Изви`ните [izv'i`n'it'e] (polite) / Изви`ни [izv'i`n'i] (informal)

9. I am sorry – Прос`тите [prʌs`t'it'e] (polite) / Прос`ти [prʌs`t'i] (informal)

10. Hi – При`вет [p`r'iv'et] (informal)

11. Hello – Зд`равствуйте [zd`rʌstvʊjt'e] (polite) / Зд`равствуй [zd`rʌstvʊj] (informal)

12. Good morning – `Доброе `утро [`dɒbrʌje `ʊtrʌ]

13. Good afternoon – `Добрый день [`dɒbryj d'en']

14. Good evening – `Добрый `вечер [`dɒbryj `v'etʃ'er]

15. Good night – Спо`койной `ночи [spʌ`kɒjnʌj `nɒtʃ'i]

16. Nice to meet you – При`ятно позна`комиться [pri`jʌtnʌ pʌznʌ`kɒm'itsʌ]

17. Welcome - Доб`ро по`жаловать [dʌbrɒ pʌ`ʒʌlʌvʌt']

18. I am glad to see you - Рад [rʌd] (masculine) / `Рада [`rʌdʌ] / `Рады [`rʌdy] вас [vʌs] (polite) / те`бя [te`b'ʌ] (informal) `видеть [`v'id'et']

19. Bless you - Будь здо`ров [bʊd' zdʌ`rɒf] (addressing a man) / Будь здо`рова (addressing a woman) [bʊd' zdʌ`rɒvʌ] / `Будьте здо`ровы [`bʊt'e zdʌ`rɒvy] (addressing several people or one person politely)

20. Come in - Прохо`дите [prʌhʌ`d'it'e] (polite) / Прохо`ди [prʌhʌ`d'i] (informal)

21. How are you? - Как де`ла? [kʌk d'e`lʌ]

22. Perfect - От`лично [ʌt`l'itʃnʌ]

23. Good - Хоро`шо [hʌrʌ`ʃɒ]

24. Bad - `Плохо [p`lɒhʌ]

25. Goodbye - До сви`дания [dʌsv'i`dʌn'ijʌ]

26. Bye - По`ка [pʌ`kʌ] (informal)

27. See you - До вст`речи [dʌvs`tr'etʃ'i]

28. Good luck - У`дачи [ʊ`dʌtʃ'i]

29. I am late - Я о`паздываю [jʌ ʌ`pʌzdyvʌjʊ]

30. I need to go - Мне `нужно ид`ти [mn'e `nʊʒnʌ it'i]

31. May I come in? - `Можно вой`ти? [`mɒʒnʌ vʌj`t'i]

32. May I stay here? - `Можно мне ос`таться здесь? [`mɒʒnʌ mn'e ʌs`tʌtsʌ zd'es']

33. Wait - Подож`дите (polite / plural) [pʌdʌʒ`d'it'e] / Подож`ди (informal) [pʌdʌʒ`d'i]

34. Wait for a second, please - Подож`дите (polite / plural) [pʌdʌʒ`d'it'e] // Подо`жди (informal)

секундочку, по`жалуйста [pʌdʌʒ`d'ɪ se`kʊndʌtʃkʊ pʌ`ʒʌlʊstʌ]

35. Is everything OK? - Всё в по`рядке? [vs'e f pʌ`r'ʌdk'e]

36. Everything is OK - Всё в по`рядке [vs'e f pʌ`r'ʌdk'e]

37. Help me, please - Помо`гите (polite / plural) [pʌmʌ`g'i] / Помо`ги (informal), по`жалуйста [pʌmʌ`g'it'e pʌ`ʒʌlʊstʌ]

38. I need help - Мне нуж`на `помощь [mn'e nʊʒ`nʌ `pɒmʌʃ']

39. What nice / terrible weather! - Ка`кая хо`рошая / у`жасная по`года! [kʌ`kʌjʌ hʌ`rɒʃʌjʌ / ʊ`ʒʌsnʌjʌ pʌ`gɒdʌ]

40. What a great day! - Ка`кой заме`чательный день! [kʌ`kɒj zʌm'e`tʃʌt'el'nyj d'en']

41. I think that... - Я `думаю, что... [jʌ `dʊmʌjʊ tʃtʌ...]

42. I agree - Я сог`ласен (masculine) [jʌ sʌg`lʌs'en] / сог`ласна (feminine) [sʌ`glʌsnʌ]

43. I disagree - Я не сог`ласен [jʌ n'e sʌg`lʌs'en] (masculine) / не сог`ласна (feminine) [n'e sʌ`glʌsnʌ]

44. You are right - Вы п`равы (polite / plural) [ʊy `prʌvy] / Ты прав (informal / masculine) [ty prʌf] / Ты пра`ва (informal / feminine) [ty prʌ`vʌ]

45. You are wrong - Вы неп`равы (polite / plural) [ʊy n'e`prʌvy] / Ты неп`рав (informal / masculine) [ty n'e prʌf] / Ты непра`ва (informal / feminine) [ty n'e prʌ`vʌ]

46. I do not care - Мне всё рав`но [mn'e fs'e rʌv`nɒ]

47. It does not matter – `Это не и`меет зна`чения [`etʌ n'e i`m'ejet znʌ`tʃen'ijʌ]

48. OK – `Ладно [`lʌdnʌ]

49. Because – Пото`му что [pʌtʌ`muʃtʌ]

50. And – И [i]

51. Or – `Или [`il'i]

52. But – Но [nɒ]

53. I know – Я `знаю [jʌ `znʌju]

54. I don't know – Я не `знаю [jʌ n'e `znʌju]

55. Tell me please – Ска`жите (polite) [skʌ`ʒit'e] / Ска`жи, по`жалуйста [skʌ`ʒi pʌ`ʒʌlustʌ]

56. Show me please – Пока`жите (polite) [pʌkʌ`ʒit'e] / Пока`жи, по`жалуйста [pʌkʌ`ʒi pʌ`ʒʌlustʌ]

57. Please, hold the door – Придер`жите (polite) [pr'id'er`ʒit'e] / Придер`жи (informal) дверь, по`жалуйста [pr'id'er`ʒit'e dv'er' pʌ`ʒʌlustʌ]

58. Open the window please – Отк`ройте (polite) [ʌtk`rɒjt'e] / Отк`рой (informal) ок`но, по`жалуйста [ʌtk`rɒj ʌk`nɒ pʌ`ʒʌlustʌ]

59. Close the window please – Зак`ройте (polite) [zʌk`rɒjt'e] / Зак`рой (informal) ок`но, по`жалуйста [zʌk`rɒj ʌk`nɒ pʌ`ʒʌlustʌ]

60. Do not stand in my way – Не ме`шайте (polite) [n'e me`ʃʌjt'e] / Не ме`шай (informal) мне [n'e me`ʃʌj mn'e]

61. Leave me alone – Ос`тавьте (polite) [ʌs`tʌft'e] / Ос`тавь (informal) ме`ня в по`кое [ʌs`tʌf' m'en'ʌ f pʌ`kɒje]

62. Let me pass, please – **Пропус`тите** (polite) [prʌpʊs`t'it'e] / **Пропус`ти** (informal) **ме`ня, по`жалуйста** [prʌpʊs`t'i me`n'ʌ, pʌ`ʒʌlʊstʌ]

63. Pleasetell me where the toilet is – **Ска`жите, по`жалуйста, где туа`лет?** [skʌ`ʒit'e pʌ`ʒʌlʊstʌ gd'e tʊʌ`l'et]

64. I am travelling alone – **Я путе`шествую о`дин** (masculine) [jʌ pʊt'e`ʃestvʊjʊ ʌ`d'in] / **од`на** (feminine) [ʌd`nʌ]

65. We are travelling together – **Мы путе`шествуем в`месте** [my pʊt'e`ʃestvʊjem v`m'est'e]

66. Where? – **Где?** [gd'e]

67. What? – **Что?** [ʃtɒ]

68. When? – **Ког`да?** [kʌg`dʌ]

69. How? – **Как?** [Kʌk]

70. How much / how many? – **С`колько?** [s`kɒl'kʌ]

3.2. Language and Making Yourself Understood

71. What did you say? – **Что вы ска`зали?** (polite / plural) [ʃtʌ vy skʌ`zʌl'i] / **Что ты ска`зал?** (informal / masculine) / **ска`зала?** (informal / feminine) [ʃtʌ ty skʌ`zʌl / skʌ`zʌlʌ]

72. Repeat, please – **Повто`рите** (polite / plural) / **Повто`ри, по`жалуйста** (informal) [pʌftʌ`r'it'e / pʌftʌ`r'i pʌ`ʒʌlʊstʌ]

73. Slowly, please – **По`медленнее, по`жалуйста** [pʌ`m'edl'en'eje pʌ`ʒʌlʊstʌ]

74. I don't speak Russian – **Я не гово`рю по-`русски** [jʌ n'e gʌvʌ`r'ʊ pʌ`rʊsk'i]

75. I speak a little bit of Russian – **Я нем`ного гово`рю по-`русски** [jʌ n'em`nɒgʌ gʌvʌ`r'ʊ pʌ`rʊsk'i]

76. I speak Russian badly – **Я п`лохо гово`рю по-`русски** [jʌ p`lɒhʌ gʌvʌ`r'ʊ pʌ`rʊsk'i]

77. I speak English – **Я гово`рю по-анг`лийски** [jʌ gʌvʌ`r'ʊ pʌ ʌng`l'ijsk'i]

78. I speak only English – **Я гово`рю `только по-анг`лийски** [jʌ gʌvʌ`r'ʊ `tɒl'kʌ pʌ ʌng`l'ijsk'i]

79. Do you speak English? – **Вы гово`рите по-анг`лийски?** [vy gʌvʌ`r'it'e pʌ ʌng`l'ijsk'i] (polite / plural) / **Ты гово`ришь по-анг`лийски?** (informal) [ty gʌvʌ`r'iʃ pʌ ʌng`l'ijsk'i]

80. Do you understand me? – **Вы пони`маете ме`ня?** [ʊy pʌn'i`mʌjet'e m'e`n'ʌ]

81. I understand – **Я пони`маю** [jʌ pʌn'i`mʌjʊ]

82. I don't understand – **Я не пони`маю** [jʌ n'e pʌn'i`mʌjʊ]

83. What does this mean? – **Что `это з`начит?** [ʃtɒ `etʌ z`nʌtʃ'it]

84. What does ... mean? – **Что з`начит ...?** [ʃtɒ z`nʌtʃ'it ...]

85. How do you say ... in Russian? – **Как `будет по-`русски ...?** [Kʌk `bʊd'et pʌ`rʊsk'ɪ ...]

86. Please, speak Russian / English – **По`жалуйста, гово`рите по-`русски / по-анг`лийски** [pʌ`ʒʌlʊstʌ gʌvʌ`r'it'e pʌ`rʊsk'ɪ / pʌ ʌng`l'ijsk'i]

87. Does anybody speak English here? – **Здесь `кто-нибудь гово`рит по-анг`лийски?** [zd'es' `ktɒn'ibʊd' gʌvʌ`r'it pʌ ʌng`l'ijsk'i]

3.3. Talking on the Phone

88. Hello [on the phone] – Ал`ло [ʌ`lɒ]

89. Who is talking? – Кто гово`рит? [Ktɒ gʌvʌ`r'it]

90. This is ... calling – `Это ... зво`нит [`etʌ ... zvʌ`n'it]

91. I cannot talk now – Не мо`гу сей`час гово`рить [n'e mʌ`gʊ sej`tʃʌs gʌvʌ`r'it']

92. I'll call you back later – Я перезво`ню по`позже [jʌ p'er'ezvʌ`n'ʊ pʌ`pɒʒe]

93. Please, call me back – По`жалуйста, перезво`ните (polite) / перезво`ни (informal) мне [pʌ`ʒʌlʊstʌ p'er'ezvʌ`n'it'e / p'er'ezvʌ`n'i mn'e]

94. Where are you? – Где вы? (polite) / ты? (informal) [gd'e vy / ty]

95. I cannot hear you – Я не с`лышу вас (polite) / те`бя (informal) [jʌ n'e `slyʃʊ vʌs / t'e`b'ʌ]

96. Speak up, please – Гово`рите (polite) / Гово`ри (informal) г`ромче, по`жалуйста [gʌvʌ`r'it'e / gʌvʌ`r'i g`rɒmtʃ'e pʌ`ʒʌlʊstʌ]

97. Speak more quietly, please – Гово`рите (polite) / Гово`ри (informal) `тише, по`жалуйста [gʌvʌ`r'it'e / gʌvʌ`r'i `tiʃe pʌ`ʒʌlʊstʌ]

98. Listen to me, please – Пос`лушайте (polite) / Пос`лушай (informal) ме`ня, по`жалуйста [pʌs`lʊʃʌjt'e / pʌs`lʊʃʌj m'e`nʌ pʌ`ʒʌlʊstʌ]

99. Thanks for calling me – Спа`сибо, что позво`нили (polite) / позво`нил (informal, addressing a man) / позво`нила (informal, addressing a woman) [spʌ`s'ibʌ ʃtʌ pʌzvʌ`n'il'i / pʌzvʌ`n'il / pʌzvʌ`n'ilʌ]

100. Thanks for calling me back – Спа`сибо, что перезво`нили (polite) / перезво`нил (informal,

addressing a man) / **перезво`нила** (informal, addressing a woman) [spʌ`s'ibʌ ʃtʌ p'e'rezvʌ`n'il'i / p'er'ezvʌ`n'il / p'er'ezvʌ`n'ilʌ]

101. Don't call me anymore - **`Больше не зво`ните** (polite) / **не зво`ни** (informal) **мне** [`bɒl'ʃe n'e zvʌ`n'it'e / n'e zvʌn'i mn'e]

102. My telephone number is ... - **Мой `номер ...** [mɒj `nɒm'er] - see **Numerals**

103. Give me your phone number please - **`Дайте** (polite) / **/Дай** (informal) **по`жалуйста, ваш / твой `номер** [`dʌjt'e / dʌj pʌ`ʒʌlustʌ vʌʃ / tvɒj `nɒmer]

3.4. Documents

104. I have ... - **У ме`ня есть ...** [u me`n'ʌ jest' ...]

105. ... Visa - **`Виза** [`v'izʌ]

106. ... Driver's licence - **Во`дительские пра`ва** [vʌ`d'it'el'sk'ije prʌ`vʌ]

107. ... Passport - **`Паспорт** [`pʌspʌrt]

108. Hand over your passport, please - **Пере`дайте ваш `паспорт, по`жалуйста** [p'er'e`dʌjt'e vʌʃ 'pʌspʌrt pʌ`ʒʌlustʌ]

109. Show your ID, please - **Пока`жите доку`менты, по`жалуйста** [pʌ`kʌʒit'e dʌku`m'enty pʌ`ʒʌlustʌ]

110. A name - **`Имя** [`ım'ʌ]

111. A surname - **Фа`милия** [fʌ`m'il'ijʌ]

112. A date of birth - **`Дата рож`дения** [`dʌtʌ rʌʒ`d'en'ijʌ]

113. A signature - **`Подпись** [`pɒdp'is']

114. Sign here - **Распи`шитесь здесь** [rʌsp'i`ʃit'es' zd'es']

115. An application - **Заяв`ление** [zʌjʌv`l'en'ije]

116. I want to submit an application - **Я хо`чу по`дать заяв`ление** [jʌ hʌ`tʃʊ pʌ`dʌt' zʌjʌv`l'en'ije]

117. Papers - **Бу`маги** [bʊ`mʌg'i]

118. Photo - **Фотог`рафия** [fʌtʌg`rʌf'ijʌ]

Chapter 4. Talking About Yourself

4.1. Introducing Yourself

119. What is your name? - **Как вас** (polite) / **тебя** (informal) **зовут?** [Kʌk vʌs / t′e`bʌ zʌ`vʊt]

120. My name is ... - **Ме`ня зо`вут ...** [m′e`n′ʌ zʌ`vʊt ...]

121. Who is that? - **Кто `это?** [Ktɒ `etʌ]

122. This is ... - **`Это ...** [`etʌ ...]

123. Do we know each other? - **Мы зна`комы?** [my znʌ`kɒmy]

124. Do you know each other? - **Вы зна`комы друг с д`ругом?** [ʊy znʌ`kɒmy drʊk s d`rʊgʌm]

125. Yes, we have met - **Да, мы зна`комы** [dʌ my znʌ`kɒmy]

126. No, we have not met - **Нет, мы не зна`комы** [n′et my n′e znʌ`kɒmy]

127. Yes, I know him / her - **Да, я е`го / её з`наю** [dʌ jʌ je`vɒ / je`jɒ `znʌjʊ]

128. No, I do not know him / her - **Нет, я е`го / её не з`наю** [n′et jʌ je`vɒ / je`jɒ n′e z`nʌʊ]

129. Let's get acquainted - **Да`вайте позна`комимся** [dʌ`vʌjt′e pʌznʌ`kɒm′ims′ʌ]

130. Please, get acquainted - this is - **Позна`комьтесь, `Это ...** [pʌznʌ`kɒm′t′es′, `etʌ ...]

131. How old are you? - **С`колько вам** (polite) / **те`бе** (informal) **лет?** [s`kɒl′kʌ vʌm / t′e`b′e l′et]

132. I am ... - **Мне ...** [mn′e ...]

- After any numeral ending with 1 – except 11 – **год** [gɒt]

- Nouns after any numeral ending with 2, 3, 4 – except 12, 13, 14 – **ˋгода** [ˈgɒdʌ]

- Nouns after the numerals 11-14 or any numeral ending with 0, 5, 6, 7, 8, 9 – **лет** [lʹet] **See Numerals**

133. I am / We are ... – **Я / Мы ...** [jʌ / my ...]

Note that in the list below, the nationalities are given in the following order – **Masculine – Feminine – Plural**

134. ... American – **Амери ˋканец – амери ˋканка – амери ˋканцы** [ʌmʹerʹiˋkʌnʹets – ʌmʹerʹiˋkʌnkʌ – ʌmʹerʹiˋkʌntsy]

135. ... Argentinian – **Арген ˋтинец – арген ˋтинка – арген ˋтинцы** [ʌrgʹenˋtʹinʹets – ʌrgʹenˋtʹinkʌ – ʌrgʹenˋtʹintsy]

136. ... Australian – **Австра ˋлиец – австра ˋлийка – австра ˋлийцы** [ʌvstrʌˋlijets – ʌvstrʌˋlijkʌ – ʌvstrʌˋlijtsy]

137. ... Belgian – **Бель ˋгиец – бель ˋгийка – бель ˋгийцы** [bʹelʹˋgʹijets – bʹelʹˋgʹijkʌ – bʹelʹˋgʹijtsy]

138. ... Brazilian – **Бра ˋзилец – брази ˋльянка – бра ˋзильцы** [brʌˋzʹilʹets – brʌzʹilˋjʌnkʌ – brʌˋzʹilʹtsy]

139. ... Canadian – **Ка ˋнадец – ка ˋнадка – ка ˋнадцы** [kʌˋnʌdʹets – kʌˋnʌtkʌ – kʌˋnʌtsy]

140. ... Chinese – **Ки ˋтаец – кита ˋянка – ки ˋтайцы** [kʹiˋtʌjets – kʹitʌˋjʌnkʌ – kʹiˋtʌjtsy]

141. ... Danish – **Дат ˋчанин – дат ˋчанка – дат ˋчане** [dʌˋtʃʌnʹin – dʌˋtʃʌnkʌ – dʌˋtʃʌnʹe]

142. ... Dutch – **Гол ˋландец – гол ˋландка – гол ˋландцы** [gʌˋlʌndʹets gʌˋlʌnkʌ – gʌˋlʌntsy]

143. ... English - **Англи`чанин - англи`чанка - англи`чане** [ʌngl'i`tʃʌn'in - ʌngl'i`tʃʌnkʌ - ʌngl'i`tʃʌn'e]

144. ... Finnish - **Финн - `финнка - `финны** [f'in - `f'inkʌ - `f'iny]

145. ... French - **Фран`цуз - фран`цуженка - фран`цузы** [frʌn`tsʊz - frʌn`tsʊʒenkʌ - frʌn`tsʊzy]

146. ... German - **`Немец - `немка - `немцы** [`n'em'ets - `n'emkʌ - `n'emtsy]

147. ... Indian - **Ин`диец - инди`анка - ин`дийцы** [ɪn`d'ijets - ind'i`ʌnkʌ - in`d'ijtsy]

148. ... Irish - **Ир`ландец - ир`ландка - ир`ландцы** [ɪr`lʌnd'ets - ir`lʌnkʌ - ir`lʌntsy]

149. ... Israeli - **Израиль`тянин - израиль`тянка - израиль`тяне** [ɪzrʌil'`t'ʌn'in - izrʌil'`t'ʌnkʌ - izrʌil'`t'ʌn'e]

150. ... Italian - **Ита`льянец - ита`льянка - ита`льянцы** [ɪtʌ`l'jʌn'ets - itʌ`l'jʌnkʌ - itʌ`l'jʌntsy]

151. ... Japanese - **Я`понец - я`понка - я`понцы** [jʌ`pɒn'ets - ʌ`pɒnkʌ - ʌ`pɒntsy]

152. ... Korean - **Ко`реец - коре`янка - ко`рейцы** [kʌ`r'ejets - kʌr'e`jʌnkʌ - kʌ`r'ejtsy]

153. ... Mexican - **Мекси`канец - мекси`канка - мекси`канцы** [m'eks'i`kʌn'ets - m'eks'i`kʌnkʌ - m'eks'i`kʌntsy]

154. ... Norwegian - **Нор`вежец - нор`вежка - нор`вежцы** [nʌr`v'eʒets - nʌr`v'eʃkʌ - nʌr`v'eʃtsy]

155. ... Polish - **По`ляк - по`лячка - по`ляки** [pʌ`l'ʌk - pʌ`l'ʌtʃkʌ - pʌ`l'ʌk'i]

156. ... Russian `Русский - `русская - `русские [`rʊskij - `rʊskʌjʌ - `rʊsk′ie]

157. ... Spanish Ис`панец - ис`панка - ис`панцы [ɪs`pʌn′ets - is`pʌnkʌ - is`pʌntsy]

158. ... Swedish Швед - ш`ведка - `шведы [ʃv′ed - ʃ`v′edkʌ - `ʃv′edy]

159. ... Turkish - `Турок - тур`чанка - `турки [`tʊrʌk - tʊr`tʃʌnkʌ - `tʊrk′i]

160. ... Ukrainian - Укра`инец - укра`инка - укра`инцы [ʊkrʌ`in′ets - ʊkrʌ`inkʌ - ʊkrʌ`intsy]

4.2. Family and Relationships

161. I have got a family - У ме`ня есть се`мья [ʊ m′e`n′ʌ jest′ s′e`mjʌ]

162. Have you got a family? - У вас (polite) / те`бя (informal) есть се`мья? [ʊ vʌs / t′e`b′ʌ jest′ s′e`mjʌ]

163. I am an only child - Я е`динственный ре`бёнок [jʌ je`d′instv′enyj r′e`b′ɒnʌk]

164. Have you got ...? - У вас (polite) / те`бя (informal) есть ...? [ʊ vʌs / t′e`b′ʌ jest′...]

165. I have got a ... - У ме`ня есть ... [ʊ m′e`n′ʌ jest′...]

166. ... Mother - Мать [mʌt′]

167. ... Father - О`тец [ʌ`t′ets]

168. ... Sister - Сест`ра [s′est`rʌ]

- After any numeral ending with 1 - except 11 - сест`ра [s′est`rʌ]

- After any numeral ending with 2, 3, 4 - except 12, 13, 14 - `сёстры [`s′ɒstry]

- After the numerals 11-14 or any numeral ending with 0, 5, 6, 7, 8, 9 – **сес`тёр** [s´es`tɒr]

See Numerals

    169. ... Brother – **Брат** [brʌt]

- After any numeral ending with 1 – except 11 – **брат** [brʌt]

- After any numeral ending with 2, 3, 4 – except 12, 13, 14 – **б`рата** [`brʌtʌ]

- After the numerals 11-14 or any numeral ending with 0, 5, 6, 7, 8, 9 – **б`ратьев** [`brʌt'jef]

See Numerals

    170. ... Grandmother – **`Бабушка** [`bʌbuʃkʌ]

    171. ... Grandfather – **`Дедушка** [`d´eduʃkʌ]

    172. ... Cousin – **Дво`юродный брат** (masculine) / **Дво`юродная сестра** (feminine) – [dvʌ`jurʌdnyj brʌt / dvʌ`jurʌdnʌjʌ s´est`rʌ]

    173. ... Uncle – **`Дядя** [`d´ʌd'ʌ]

    174. ... Aunt – **`Тётя** [`t´ɒt'ʌ]

    175. ... Daughter – **Дочь** [dɒtʃ']

- After any numeral ending with 1 – except 11 – **дочь** [dɒtʃ']

- After any numeral ending with 2, 3, 4 – except 12, 13, 14 – **`дочери** [`dɒtʃ'er'i]

- After the numerals 11-14 or any numeral ending with 0, 5, 6, 7, 8, 9 – **доче`рей** [dʌtʃ'e`r'ej]

See Numerals

    176. ... Son – **Сын** [syn]

- After any numeral ending with 1 – except 11 – **сын** [syn]

- After any numeral ending with 2, 3, 4 – except 12, 13, 14 – **`сына** [`synʌ]

- After the numerals 11-14 or any numeral ending with 0, 5, 6, 7, 8, 9 – **сыно`вей** [synʌ`v'ej]

See Numerals

    177. ... Wife – **Же`на** [ʒe`nʌ]

    178. ... Husband – **Муж** [mʊʒ]

    179. ... Grandson – **Внук** [vnʊk]

- After any numeral ending with 1 – except 11 – **внук** [vnʊk`]

- After any numeral ending with 2, 3, 4 – except 12, 13, 14 – **`внука** [v`nʊkʌ]

- After the numerals 11-14 or any numeral ending with 0, 5, 6, 7, 8, 9 – **`внуков** [v`nʊkʌf]

See Numerals

    180. ... Granddaughter – **`Внучка** [`vnʊtʃ'kʌ]

- After any numeral ending with 1 – except 11 – **`внучка** [`vnʊtʃ'kʌ]

- After any numeral ending with 2, 3, 4 – except 12, 13, 14 – **`внучки** [`vnʊtʃ'k'i]

- After the numerals 11-14 or any numeral ending with 0, 5, 6, 7, 8, 9 – **`внучек** [`vnʊtʃ'ek]

See Numerals

    181. ... Nephew – **Пле`мянник** [pl'e`m'ʌn'ik]

    182. ... Niece – **Пле`мянница** [pl'e`m'ʌn'itsʌ]

    183. ... Boyfriend – **`Парень** [`pʌr'en']

184. ... Girlfriend - `Девушка [`d′evuʃkʌ]

185. ... Fiancé - Же`них (masculine) / Не`веста (feminine) [ʒe′n′ih / n′e`v′estʌ]

186. ... Friend - Друг [druk]

187. ... Best friend - `Лучший друг [`lutʃʃij druk]

188. I am the eldest child - Я с`таршиӣ (masculine) / с`таршая (feminine) в се`мье [jʌ s`tʌrʃij / s`tʌrʃʌjʌ v s′emje]

189. I am the youngest child - Я м`ладший (masculine) / м`ладшая (feminine) в се`мье [jʌ m`lʌdʃij / m`lʌdʃʌjʌ v s′e`mje]

190. Are you married? - Вы же`наты? (polite, masculine) [υy ʒe`nʌty] / Ты же`нат? (informal, masculine) [ty ʒenʌt] / Вы `замужем? (polite, feminine) [vy `zʌmuʒem] / Ты `замужем? (informal, feminine) [ty `zʌmuʒem]

191. Have you got any children? - У вас (polite) / те`бя есть `дети? [υ vʌs / t′e`b′ʌ jest′ `d′et′i]

192. How many children have you got? - С`колько у вас (polite) / те`бя (informal) де`тей? [s`kɒl′kʌ υ vʌs / t′e`b′ʌ d′e`t′ej]

193. Have you got any siblings? - У вас (polite) / те`бя (informal) есть б`ратья и `сёстры? [υ vʌs / t′e`b′ʌ jest′ b`rʌt′jʌ i `sɒstry]

194. I am married - Я же`нат (masculine) / `замужем (feminine) [jʌ ʒe`nʌt / `zʌmuʒem]

195. I am not married - Я не же`нат (masculine) / не `замужем (feminine) [jʌ n′e ʒe`nʌt / n′e `zʌmuʒem]

196. I am divorced - Я разве`дён (masculine) / разведе`на (feminine) [jʌ rʌz`v′e`d′ɒn / rʌzv′ed′e`nʌ]

4.3. Professions and Occupations

197. What do you do for a living? - **Кем вы ра`ботаете** (polite) **/ ты ра`ботаешь?** (informal) [kʹem vy rʌ`bɒtʌjetʹe / ty rʌ`bɒtʌjeʃ]

198. I am [a / an] ... - **Я ...** [jʌ ...]

199. ... Accountant - **Бух`галтер** [bʊ`gʌltʹer]

200. ... Actor / Actress - **Ак`тёр / Акт`риса** [ʌk`tʹɒr / ʌktʹrʹisʌ]

201. ... Administrator - **Админист`ратор** [ʌdmʹinʹistʹ`rʌtʌr]

202. ... Analyst - **Ана`литик** [ʌnʌ`lʹitʹik]

203. ... Architect - **Архи`тектор** [ʌrhʹiʹtʹektʌr]

204. ... Archeologist - **Архе`олог** [ʌrhʹeʹɒlʌg]

205. ... Artist - **Ху`дожник** [hʊ`dɒʒnʹik]

206. ... Assistant - **Ассис`тент** [ʌsʹisʹtʹent]

207. ... Author - **Пи`сатель** [pʹiʹsʌtʹelʹ]

208. ... Biologist - **Би`олог** [bʹiʹɒlʌg]

209. ... Builder - **Стро`итель** [strʌ`itʹelʹ]

210. ... Businessman - **Бизнес`мен** [bʹizneʹsʹmen]

211. ... Cameraman - **Опе`ратор** [ʌpʹeʹrʌtʌr]

212. ... Chemist - **`Химик** [`hʹimʹik]

213. ... Civil servant - **Чи`новник** [tʃiʹnɒvnʹik]

214. ... Computer programmer - **Програм`мист** [prʌgrʌ`mʹist]

215. ... Consultant - **Консуль`тант** [kʌnsʊlʹ`tʌnt]

216. ... Cook - **`Повар** [`pɒvʌr]

217. ... Dancer - **Тан`цор** (masculine) / **Тан`цовщица** (feminine) [tʌn`tsɒr / tʌn`tsɒvʃ'itsʌ]

218. ... Designer - **Ди`зайнер** [d'izʌjn'er]

219. ... Developer [software] - **Разра`ботчик** [rʌzrʌ`bɒtʧ'ik]

220. ... Diplomat - **Дипло`мат** [d'iplʌ`mʌt]

221. ... Director - **Ди`ректор** [d'i`r'ektʌr]

222. ... Doctor - **Врач** [ʊrʌʧ]

223. ... Driver - **Во`дитель** [vʌ`d'it'el']

224. ... Economist - **Эконо`мист** [ekʌnʌ`m'ist]

225. ... Editor - **Ре`дактор** [r'e`dʌktʌr]

226. ... Electrician - **Э`лектрик** [e`l'ektr'ik]

227. ... Engineer - **Инже`нер** [ɪnʒe`n'er]

228. ... Entrepreneur - **Предприни`матель** [pr'edpr'in'i`mʌt'el']

229. ... Environmentalist - **Э`колог** [e`kɒlʌg]

230. ... Executive - **Р`уково`дитель** [rʊkʌvʌ`d'it'el']

231. ... Farmer - **`Фермер** [`f'erm'er]

232. ... Film director - **Режис`сёр** [reʒis'ɒr]

233. ... Fisherman - **Ры`бак** [ry`bʌk]

234. ... Fireman - **По`жарный** [pʌ`ʒʌrnyj]

235. ... Flight attendant - **Ст`юард** (masculine) / **стюар`десса** (feminine) [s`t'ʊʌrt / st'ʊʌr`desʌ]

236. ... Geologist - **Ге`олог** [ge`ɒlʌg]

237. ... Hairdresser - **Парик`махер** [pʌr'ik`mʌh'er]

238. ... Historian - **Ис`торик** [ɪs`tɒr'ik]

239. ... Housewife - **Домохо`зяйка** [dʌmʌhʌ`z'ʌjkʌ]

240. ... Instructor - Инст`руктор [ɪnsˈtrʊktʌr]

241. ... Jeweler - Юве`лир [jʊv′eˈl′ir]

242. ... Journalist - Журна`лист [ʒʊrnʌˈl′ist]

243. ... Lawyer - Ю`рист [jʊˈr′ist]

244. ... Lecturer [at university] - Препода`ватель [pr′epʌdʌˈvʌt′el′]

245. ... Librarian - Библио`текарь [b′ibl′iʌˈt′ekʌr′]

246. ... Makeup artist - Виза`жист [v′izʌˈʒist]

247. ... Manager - `Менеджер [ˈmenedʒer]

248. ... Mechanic - Ме`ханик [m′eˈhʌn′ik]

249. ... Military person - Во`енный [ʊʌˈjenyj]

250. ... Miner - Шах`тёр [ʃʌhˈt′ɒr]

251. ... Musician - Музы`кант [mʊzyˈkʌnt]

252. ... Nurse - Мед`брат (masculine) / медсест`ра (feminine) [m′edbˈrʌt / m′eds′estˈrʌ]

253. ... Photographer - Фо`тограф [fʌˈtɒgrʌf]

254. ... Psychologist - Пси`холог [ps′iˈhɒlʌg]

255. ... Physicist - `Физик [ˈf′iz′ik]

256. ... Pilot - `Лётчик [ˈl′ɒttʃik]

257. ... Plumber - Водопро`водчик [vʌdʌprʌˈvɒtʃ′ik]

258. ... Police officer - Поли`цейский [pʌl′itsejskij]

259. ... Politician - По`литик [pʌˈl′it′ik]

260. ... Representative - Предста`витель [pr′etstʌˈv′it′el′]

261. ... Sailor - Мо`ряк [mʌˈr′ʌk]

262. ... Salesperson - Прода`вец [prʌdʌˈv′ets]

263. ... Scientist - **У`чёный** [u`tʃ′ɒnyj]

264. ... Secretary - **Секре`тарь** [s′ekr′e`tʌr′]

265. ... Shop assistant - **Прода`вец** [prʌdʌ`v′ets]

266. ... Singer - **Пе`вец** (masculine) / **пе`вица** (feminine) [p′e`v′ets / p′e`v′itsʌ]

267. ... Sportsman - **Спортс`мен** (masculine) / **спортс`менка** (feminine) [spʌrts`m′en / spʌrts`m′enkʌ]

268. ... Student [at university] - **Сту`дент** (masculine) / **сту`дентка** (feminine) [stʋ`d′ent / stʋ`d′entkʌ]

269. ... Teacher [at school] - **У`читель** [u`tʃ′it′el′]

270. ... Vet - **Ветери`нар** [v′et′er′i`nʌr]

271. ... Waiter / waitress - **Офици`ант** / **офици`антка** [ʌf′i`tsʌnt / ʌf′i`tsʌntkʌ]

272. Where do you work? - **Где вы ра`ботаете?** (polite) / **Где ты ра`ботаешь?** (informal) [gd′e vy rʌ`bɒtʌjete / gde ty rʌ`bɒtʌjeʃ]

273. I work ... - **Я ра`ботаю ...** [jʌ rʌ`bɒtʌjʋ ...]

274. ... In an agency - **В а`гентстве** [v ʌ`g′entstv′e]

275. ... In a clinic - **В `клинике** [v k`l′in′ik′e]

276. ... In a company - **В ком`пании** [v kʌm`pʌnii]

277. ... In a hospital - **В боль`нице** [v bʌl′`nitse]

278. ... In an office - **В `офисе** [v `ɒf′is′e]

279. ... In an organization - **В органи`зации** [v ʌrgʌn′i`zʌtsii]

280. ... At school - **В ш`коле** [v ʃ`kɒl′e]

281. ... In a studio - **В `студии** [v s`tʋd′ii]

282. ... In a theater - **В те`атре** [v t′e`ʌtr′e]

283. ... At university - В университе́те [v ʊnʲivʲersʲiˈtʲetʲe]

284. I work for myself - Я рабо́таю на себя́ [jʌ rʌˈbɒtʌjʊ nʌ sʲeˈbʲʌ]

285. I am a freelancer - Я фри́лансер [jʌ frʲiˈlʌnser]

286. My company's name is ... - Моя́ компа́ния называ́ется ... [mʌˈjʌ kʌmˈpʌnʲijʌ nʌzyˈvʌjetsʌ...]

287. My organization's name is ... - Моя́ организа́ция называ́ется ... [mʌˈjʌ ʌrgʌnʲiˈzʌtsijʌ nʌzyˈvʌjetsʌ...]

288. I don't work - Я не рабо́таю [jʌ nʲe rʌˈbɒtʌjʊ]

289. I study ... - Я учу́сь в ... [jʌ ʊˈtʃʊsʲ v...]

290. ... At school - шко́ле [ʃˈkɒlʲe]

291. ... At university - университе́те [ʊnʲivʲersʲiˈtʲetʲe]

292. I am retired - Я на пе́нсии [jʌ nʌˈpʲensʲii]

293. I am looking for a job - Я ищу́ рабо́ту [jʌ iʃʊ rʌˈbɒtʊ]

4.4. Interests

294. What are you engaged in? - Чем вы занима́етесь? (polite) / Чем ты занима́ешься? (informal) [tʃʲem vy zʌnʲiˈmʌjetʲesʲ? / tʃʲem ty zʌnʲiˈmʌjeʃsʲʌ]

295. What are you interested in? - Чем вы интересу́етесь? (polite) / Чем ты интересу́ешься? (informal) [tʃʲem vy intʲerʲeˈsʊjetʲesʲ / tʃʲem ty intʲerʲeˈsʊjeʃsʲʌ]

296. I am engaged in ... - Я занима́юсь... [jʌ zʌnʲiˈmʌjʊsʲ...]

297. I am not engaged in ... - **Я не зани`маюсь...** [jʌ n'e zʌn'i`mʌjʊs'...]

298. I am interested in ... - **Я интере`суюсь** ... [jʌ int'er'e`sʊjʊs' ...]

299. I am not interested in - **Я не интере`суюсь** ... [jʌ n'e int'er'e`sʊjʊs' ...]

300. ... Art - **Ис`кусством** [ɪs`kʊstvʌm]

301. ... Biology - **Био`логией** [bɪʌ`lɒgijej]

302. ... Business - **`Бизнесом** [`b'ɪznesʌm]

303. ... Engineering - **`Техникой** [`t'ehn'ikʌj]

304. ... Environmental studies - **Эко`логией** [ekʌ`lɒgijej]

305. ... History - **Ис`торией** [ɪs`tɒriej]

306. ... Journalism - **Журна`листикой** [ʒʊrnʌ`l'ist'ikʌj]

307. ... Languages - **Язы`ками** [ʌzy`kʌm'i]

308. ... Literature - **Литера`турой** [l'it'erʌ`tʊrʌj]

309. ... Mathematics - **Мате`матикой** [mʌt'e`mʌt'ikʌj]

310. ... Medicine - **Меди`циной** [m'ed'i`tsinʌj]

311. ... Science - **На`укой** [ŋʌ`ʊkʌj]

312. ... Sport - **С`портом** [s`pɒrtʌm]

313. ... Physics - **`Физикой** [`f'iz'ikʌj]

314. ... Photography - **Фотог`рафией** [fʌtʌg`rʌfijej]

315. ... Poetry - **По`эзиией** [pʌ`ezijej]

316. ... Politics - **По`литикой** [pʌ`l'it'ikʌj]

317. ... Psychology - **Психо`логией** [ps'ihʌ`lɒgijej]

318. What are your hobbies? - **Ка`кие у те`бя** (informal) **/ вас** (polite) **увле`чения?** [kʌ`k'ije ʊ t'e`b'ʌ / vʌs ʊvl'e`tʃen'ijʌ]

319. I enjoy ... - **Я люб`лю ...** [jʌ lʊb`l'ʊ]

320. ... Cooking - **Го`товить** [gʌ`tɒv'it']

321. ... Cycling - **Ка`таться на велоси`педе** [kʌ`tʌtsʌ nʌ v'elʌs'i`p'ed'e]

322. ... Dancing - **Танце`вать** [tʌntse`vʌt']

323. ... Diving - **Ны`рять** [ŋy`r'ʌt']

324. ... Doing yoga - **Зани`маться `йогой** [zʌn'i`mʌtsʌ `jɒgʌj]

325. ... Drawing / Painting - **Рисо`вать** [r'isʌ`vʌt']

326. ... Fishing - **Ры`бачить** [ry`bʌtʃ'it']

327. ... Gardening - **Ра`ботать в са`ду** [rʌ`bɒtʌt' v sʌ`dʊ]

328. ... Horse riding - **`Ездить вер`хом** [jezd'it' v'er`hɒm]

329. ... Listening to music - **С`лушать `музыку** [s`lʊʃʌt' `mʊzykʊ]

330. ... Playing computer games - **Иг`рать в ком`пьютерные `игры** [ɪg`rʌt' v kʌmpjʊternyje `igry]

331. ... Reading - **Чи`тать** [tʃi`tʌt']

332. ... Running - **`Бегать** [`b'egʌt']

333. ... Sailing - **Хо`дить под `парусом** [hʌd'it' pʌd `pʌrʊsʌm]

334. ... Skating - **Ка`таться на конь`ках** [kʌ`tʌtsʌ nʌ kʌn'kʌh]

335. ... Skiing - **Ка`таться на `лыжах** [kʌ`tʌtsʌ nʌ `lyʒʌh]

336. ... Swimming - Пла́вать [pˈlʌvʌtʲ]

337. ... Taking walks - Гуля́ть [gʊˈlʌtʲ]

338. ... Traveling - Путеше́ствовать [pʊtʲeˈʃestvʌvʌtʲ]

339. ... Watching films - Смотре́ть фи́льмы [smʌtˈrʲetʲ ˈfʲilʲmy]

340. Do you like ...? - Вам (polite) / Тебе́ (informal) нра́вится ...? [vʌm / tʲeˈbʲe nˈrʌvʲitsʌ ...]

341. I like - Мне нра́вится ... [mnʲe nˈrʌvʲitsʌ ...]

342. ... Architecture - Архитекту́ра [ʌrhʲitʲekˈtʊrʌ]

343. ... Art - Иску́сство [ɪsˈkʊstvʌ]

344. ... Ballet - Бале́т [bʌˈlʲet]

345. ... Ceramics - Кера́мика [kʲeˈrʌmʲikʌ]

346. ... Cinema - Кино́ [kʲiˈnɒ]

347. ... Music - Му́зыка [ˈmʊzykʌ]

348. ... Opera - О́пера [ˈɒpʲerʌ]

349. ... Nature - Приро́да [prʲiˈrɒdʌ]

350. ... Painting - Жи́вопись [ˈʒivʌpʲisʲ]

351. ... Sculpture - Скульпту́ра [skʊlʲpˈtʊrʌ]

352. ... Sport - Спорт [spɒrt]

353. ... Theater - Теа́тр [tʲeˈʌtr]

354. Do you collect anything? - Вы (polite) / Ты (informal) коллекционе́р? [ty / ʊy kʌlʲektsiʌˈnʲer]

355. I collect ... - Я собира́ю ... [jʌ sʌbʲiˈrʌjʊ ...]

356. ... Antiques - Антиквариа́т [ʌntʲikvʌrʲiˈʌt]

357. ... Autographs - Авто́графы [ʌfˈtɒgrʌfy]

358. ... Coins - Моне́ты [mʌˈnʲety]

359. ... Comic books - `Комиксы [`kɒm'iksy]

360. ... Books - К`ниги [k`n'ig'i]

361. ... Figurines - Фи`гурки [f'i`gʊrk'i]

362. ... Paintings - Кар`тины [kʌr`t'iny]

363. ... Stamps - `Марки [`mʌrk'i]

364. ... Toys - Иг`рушки [ıg`rʊʃk'i]

365. Do you like any sport? - Вам (polite) / Тебе (informal) н`равится спорт? [ʋam / t'e`b'e n`rʌv'itsʌ spɒrt]

366. I play ... - Я иг`раю в ... [jʌ ig`rʌjʊ v ...]

367. I watch ... - Я смотрю ... [jʌ smʌt`r'ʊ ...]

368. ... Badminton - Бадмин`тон [bʌdmin`tɒn]

369. ... Baseball - Бейс`бол [b'ejs`bɒl]

370. ... Basketball - Баскет`бол [bʌsk'et`bɒl]

371. ... Chess - `Шахматы [`ʃʌhmʌty]

372. ... Football - Фут`бол [fʊt`bɒl]

373. ... Golf - Гольф [gɒl'f]

374. ... Hockey - Хок`кей [hʌ`kej]

375. ... Tennis - `Теннис [`ten'is]

376. ... Volleyball - Волей`бол [ʋʌl'ej`bɒl]

377. Do you play a musical instrument? - Вы играете (polite) / Ты играешь (informal) на музыкальных инструментах? - [ʋy ig`rʌjet'e / ty ig`rʌjeʃ nʌ mʊzy`kʌl'nyh instrʊ`m'entʌh]

378. I play ... - Я играю на ... [jʌ ig`rʌjʊ nʌ ...]

379. ... Cello - Виолон`чели [ʋiʌlʌɒn`tʃ'el'i]

380. ... Clarinet - Клар`нете [klʌr`n'et'e]

381. ... Drums – **Бара`банах** [bʌrʌ`bʌnʌh]
382. ... Flute – **Ф`лейте** [fl′ejt′e]
383. ... Guitar – **Ги`таре** [gi`tʌr′e]
384. ... Harp – **`Арфе** [`ʌrf′e]
385. ... Piano – **`Форте`пиано** [`fɒrte′pjʌnʌ]
386. ... Saxophone – **Саксо`фоне** [sʌksʌ`fɒn′e]
387. ... Trumpet – **Тру`бе** [trʊ`b′e]
388. ... Violin – **Ск`рипке** [sk`r′ipk′e]

Chapter 5. Getting Around

5.1. Airport

389. Where is Terminal …? – Где терми`нал …? [gd′e t′ermi`nʌl …] **See Numbers**

390. Where is the Departure hall? – Где зал отправ`ления? [gd′e zʌl ʌtprʌv`l′en′ijʌ]

391. Where is the Arrival hall? – Где зал при`бытия? [gd′e zʌl pr′ibyt′ijʌ]

392. Where is the arrival and departure board? – Где информаци`онное таб`ло? [gd′e infʌrmʌtsi`ɒnʌje tʌb`lɒ]

393. Where are the check-in desks? – Где с`тойки регист`рации? [gd′e s`tɒjk′i r′eg′ist`rʌtsii]

394. Where do I check in? – Где `можно зарегист`рироваться на рейс? [gd′e ′mɒʒnʌ zʌr′eg′ist`r′irʌvʌtsʌ nʌ rejs]

395. My flight number is … – У ме`ня рейс `номер … [ʊ m′e`n′ʌ rejs `nɒm′er …] **See Numbers**

396. I'd like to check-in my luggage – Я хо`чу зарегист`рировать ба`гаж [jʌ hʌ`tʃ′ʊ zʌr′eg′ist`r′irʌvʌt′ bʌ`gʌʒ]

397. I'd like a window seat, please – Мне, по`жалуйста, `место у ок`на [mn′e pʌ`ʒʌlʊstʌ `m′estʌ ʊ ʌk`nʌ]

398. I'd like an aisle seat, please – Мне, по`жалуйста, `место у про`хода [mn′e pʌ`ʒʌlʊstʌ `m′estʌ ʊ prʌ`hɒdʌ]

399. When does the boarding begin? - **Ког`да начи`нается по`садка?** [kʌg`dʌ nʌtʃ'i`nʌjetsʌ pʌ`sʌtkʌ]

400. What is my gate number? - **Ка`кие у ме`ня во`рота?** [kʌ`k'ije u m'e`n'ʌ vʌ`rɒtʌ]

401. Your gate number is ... - **У вас во`рота `номер ...** [u vʌs vʌ`rɒtʌ `nɒm'er ...] **See Numbers**

402. What is the charge for an excess kilo? - **`Сколько `нужно допла`тить за `лишний килог`рамм?** [`skɒl'kʌ `nuʒnʌ dʌplʌ`t'it' zʌ l'iʃn'ij k'ilʌg`rʌm]

403. You have to pay for excess luggage - **Вам `нужно допла`тить за пере`вес** [vʌm `nuʒnʌ dʌplʌ`t'it' zʌ p'er'e`v'es]

404. Go through the security screening please - **Прой`дите, по`жалуйста, дос`мотр** [prʌjd'it'e pʌ`ʒʌlustʌ dʌs`mɒtr]

405. This is my luggage - **`Это мой ба`гаж** [`etʌ mɒj bʌ`gʌʒ]

406. This is my suitcase - **`Это мой чемо`дан** [`etʌ mɒj tʃ'emʌdʌn]

407. This is my briefcase - **`Это мой порт`фель** [`etʌ mɒj pʌrt`f'el']

408. This is my bag - **`Это мо`я `сумка** [`etʌ mʌ`jʌ `sumkʌ]

409. This is my backpack - **`Это мой рюк`зак** [`etʌ mɒj r'uk`zʌk]

410. This is my hand luggage - **`Это мо`я руч`ная кладь** [`etʌ mʌ`jʌ rutʃ`nʌjʌ klʌd']

411. This is my pram - **`Это мо`я `детская ко`ляска** [`etʌ mʌ`jʌ d'etskʌjʌ kʌ`l'ʌskʌ]

412. Can you please let me get by, I am late! – **Пропус`тите ме`ня, по`жалуйста, впе`рёд, я о`паздываю** [prʌpus`t'it'e m'en'ʌ pʌ`ʒʌlustʌ vp'e`r'ɒt jʌ ʌ`pʌzdyvʌju]

413. Open your suitcase / bag for examination, please – **По`жалуйста, отк`ройте свой чемо`дан / сво`ю `сумку для дос`мотра** [pʌ`ʒʌlustʌ ʌtk`rɒjt'e svɒj tʃ'emʌ`dʌn / svʌ`ju `sumku dl'ʌ dʌ`smɒtrʌ]

414. Take off your shoes, please – **Сни`мите, по`жалуйста, бо`тинки** [sn'i`m'it'e pʌ`ʒʌlustʌ bʌ`t'ink'i]

415. Put your tablet / laptop / camera / phone out of your bag, please – **Дос`таньте, по`жалуйста, из `сумки план`шет / ноут`бук / фотоаппа`рат / теле`фон** [dʌs`tʌn't'e pʌ`ʒʌlustʌ 'iz `sumk'i plan`ʃet / nɒut`buk / `fɒtɒʌ`pʌrʌt / t'el'e`fɒn]

416. Take off any metallic items and put them here – **Сни`мите все метал`лические пред`меты и поло`жите их сю`да** [sn'i`m'ite vs'e m'etʌ`l'itʃ'esk'ije pr'ed`m'ety i pʌlʌ`ʒ'it'e ih s'udʌ]

417. Can I take it on board? – **`Можно взять `это в само`лёт?** [`mɒʒnʌ vz'ʌt' `etʌ v sʌmʌ`l'ɒt]

418. You can take it on board – **Вы `можете взять `это в само`лёт** [vy `mɒʒet'e vz'ʌt' `etʌ v sʌmʌ`l'ɒt]

419. You cannot take it on board – **`Это нель`зя взять в само`лёт** [`etʌ n'el'`z'ʌ vzʌt' etɒ v sʌmʌ`l'ɒt]

420. Is there anything sharp or dangerous in your hand luggage? – **В `вашей руч`ной `клади есть `острые `или о`пасные пред`меты?** [v `vʌʃej rutʃ`nɒj k`lʌd'i est' `ɒstryje il'i ʌ`pʌsnye pr'ed`m'ety]

421. When does the boarding for the flight ... start? - **Ког`да начи`нается по`садка на рейс...?** [kʌg`dʌ nʌtʃ'i`nʌjetsʌ pʌ`sʌtkʌ nʌ rejs...] **See Numbers**

422. The boarding for the flight ... will start in ... minutes - **По`садка на рейс нач`нётся `через...** [pʌ`sʌtkʌ nʌ rejs nʌtʃ`n'ɒtsʌ tʃr'ez...]

- After any numeral ending with 1 - except 11 - **ми`нуту** [m'i`nʊtʊ]

- After any numeral ending with 2, 3, 4 - except 12, 13, 14 - **мин`уты** [m'i`nʊty]

- Nouns after the numerals 11-14 or any numeral ending with 0, 5, 6, 7, 8, 9 - **ми`нут** [m'i`nʊt]

See Numerals

423. The boarding for the flight ... is now starting - **Начи`нается по`садка на рейс...** [ŋʌtʃ'i`nʌjetsʌ pʌ`sʌtkʌ nʌ rejs...] **See Numerals**

424. Is that a direct flight? - **`Это пря`мой рейс?** [`etʌ pr'ʌ`mɒj rejs]

425. Is it a connecting flight? - **`Это рейс с пере`садкой?** [`etʌ rejs s p'er'e`sʌtkʌj]

426. How long does our flight take? - **С`колько нам ле`теть?** [`skɒl'kʌ nʌm l'e`t'et']

427. Do they serve food during the flight? - **Во в`ремя по`лёта `будут кор`мить?** [vʌ v`r'em'ʌ pʌ'l'ɒtʌ `bʊdʊt kʌr`m'it']

428. Can I have a blanket, please? - **`Можно мне, по`жалуйста, плед?** ['mɒʒnʌ mn'e pʌ`ʒʌlʊstʌ pl'et]

429. Can I have some water, please? - **`Можно мне, по`жалуйста, во`ды?** ['mɒʒnʌ mn'e pʌ`ʒʌlʊstʌ vʌ`dy]

430. Could you please direct me to my seat? – **Пока`жите, по`жалуйста, мо`ё `место** [pʌkʌ`ʒ'it'e pʌ`ʒʌlʊstʌ mʌ`jɒ `m'estʌ]

431. Could I change seats with you? – **`Можно поме`няться с `вами мес`тами?** [`mɒʒnʌ pʌm'e`n'ʌtsʌ s `vʌm'i m'es`tʌm'i]

432. Welcome on board – **Доб`ро по`жаловать на борт** [dʌb`rɒ pʌ`ʒʌlʌvʌt' nʌ bɒrt]

433. Please, fasten your seat-belts – **По`жалуйста, пристег`ните рем`ни** [pʌ`ʒʌlʊstʌ pr'ist'eg`n'it'e r'em`n'i]

434. Smoking is prohibited throughout the flight – **Ку`рение во в`ремя по`лёта запреще`но** [kʊ`r'en'ije vʌ vr'e`m'ʌ pʌ'l'ɒtʌ zʌpr'eʃ'e`nɒ]

435. Please, put your chairs into an upright position – **По`жалуйста, приве`дите с`пинки к`ресел в верти`кальное поло`жение** [pʌ`ʒʌlʊstʌ pr'iv'e`d'it'e s`p'ink'i k`r'es'el v v'ert'i`kʌl'nʌje pʌlʌ`ʒen'ije]

436. I need a migration form – **Мне нуж`на мигpaци`онная `карта** [mn'e nʊʒ`nʌ m'igrʌtsi`ɒnʌjʌ `kʌrtʌ]

437. Where is the passport control? – **Где `паспортный конт`роль?** [gd'e `pʌspʌrtnyj kʌnt`rɒl']

438. What is the purpose of your visit? – **Како`ва цель `вашего при`езда?** [kʌkʌ`vʌ tsel' `vʌʃevʌ pr'i`jezdʌ]

439. ... Business – **`Бизнес** [`b'iznes]

440. ... Business trip – **Команди`ровка** [kʌmʌnd'i`rɒfkʌ]

441. ... Conference – **Конфе`ренция** [kʌnf'e`r'entsijʌ]

442. ... Medical treatment – **Ле`чение** [l'e`tʃ'en'ije]

443. ... Personal - `Личная [`l′itʃnʌjʌ]

444. ... Tourism - Ту`ризм [tʊ`r′izm]

445. I am a citizen of ... - Я гражданин ... (masculine) / гражданка ... (feminine) [jʌ grʌzdʌ`n′in / grʌʒ`dʌnkʌ ...]

446. ... Argentina - Арген`тины [ʌrg′en`t′iny]

447. ... Australia - Авст`ралии [ʌvst`rʌl′ii]

448. ... Belgium - `Бельгии [b′el′`g′ii]

449. ... Brasil - Бра`зилии [brʌ`z′il′ii]

450. ... Canada - Ка`нады [kʌ`nʌdy]

451. ... China - Ки`тая [k′i`tʌjʌ]

452. ... Denmark - `Дании [`dʌn′ii]

453. ... Finland - Фин`ляндии [f′in`l′ʌnd′ii]

454. ... France - Ф`ранции [f`rʌnts′ii]

455. ... Germany - Гер`мании [g′er`mʌn′ii]

456. ... Great Britain - Великобри`тании [v′el′ikʌbr′i`tʌn′ii]

457. ... India - `Индии [`ınd′ii]

458. ... Israel - Из`раиля [ız`rʌil′ʌ]

459. ... Italy - И`талии [ı`tʌl′ii]

460. ... Japan - Я`понии [jʌ`pɒn′ii]

461. ... Korea - Ко`реи [kʌr′ei]

462. ... Mexico - `Мексики [`m′eks′ik′i]

463. ... The Netherlands - Нидер`ландов [n′ider`lʌndʌf]

464. ... Norway - Нор`вегии [nʌr`v′eg′ii]

465. ... Poland - `Польши [`pɒl′ʃy]

466. ... Russia - **Рос`сии** [rʌ`s'ii]

467. ... Spain - **Ис`пании** [ɪs`pʌn'ii]

468. ... Sweden - **`Швеции** [ʃ`v'etsii]

469. ... Turkey - **`Турции** [`tʊrtsii]

470. ... Ukraine - **Укра`ины** [ʊkrʌ`iny]

471. ... USA - **США** [se ʃe ʌ]

472. How long are you going to stay here? - **Как `долго вы соби`раетесь здесь про`быть?** [Kʌk `dɒlgʌ vy sʌb'i`rʌjet'es' zd'es' prʌ`byt']

473. I am going to stay in the country for ... day(s) / month(s) - **Я соби`раюсь про`быть в стра`не ...** [jʌ sʌb'i`rʌjʊs' prʌ`byt' v strʌ`n'e ...]

- After any numeral ending with 1 - except 11 - **день / `месяц** [den' / `m'es'ʌts]

- After any numeral ending with 2, 3, 4 - except 12, 13, 14 - **дня / `месяца** [dn'ʌ / `m'es'ʌtsʌ]

- Nouns after the numerals 11-14 or any numeral ending with 0, 5, 6, 7, 8, 9 - **дней / `месяцев** [dn'ej / `m'es'ʌtsef]

See Numerals

474. Where are you going to stay? - **Где вы соби`раетесь остано`виться?** [gd'e vy sʌb'i`rʌjet'es' ʌstʌnʌ`v'itsʌ]

475. I'll stay in / at - **Я останов`люсь ...** [jʌ ʌstʌnʌv`l'ʊs' ...]

476. ... Hotel - **в гос`тинице** [v gʌs`t'in'itse]

477. ... Hostel - **в `хостеле** [v `hɒstel'e]

478. ... In a rented flat - **на `съёмной квар`тире** [nʌ `sjɒmnʌj kvʌr`t'ir'e]

479. ... My friends - у дру`зей [ʊ drʊ`zʼej]

480. ... My relatives - у `родственников [ʊ `rɒtstvʼenʼikʌf]

481. Where is the baggage claim? - Где полу`чают ба`гаж? [gdʼe pʌlʊ`ʧʌjʊt bʌ`gʌʒ]

482. My luggage is lost - Мой ба`гаж поте`рялся [mɒj bʌ`gʌʒ pʌtʼe`rʼʌlsʼʌ]

483. Where is the customs office? - Где та`можня? [gdʼe tʌ`mɒʒnʼʌ]

484. Are you a customs officer? - Вы ра`ботник та`можни? [ʊy rʌ`bɒtnʼik tʌ`mɒʒnʼi]

485. I need a customs declaration form - Мне `нужен бланк та`моженной декла`рации [mnʼe `nʊʒen blʌnk tʌ`mɒʒenʌj dʼeklʌ`rʌtsʼii]

486. Here is my customs declaration - Вот мо`я та`моженная декла`рация [ʊɒt mʌ`jʌ tʌ`mɒʒenʌjʌ dʼeklʌ`rʌtsijʌ]

487. Have you anything to declare? - У вас есть декла`рируемые то`вары? [ʊ vʌs jestʼ dʼeklʌ`rʼirʊjemyje tʌ`vʌry]

488. I have nothing to declare - У ме`ня нет деклари`руемых то`варов [ʊ mʼe`nʼʌ nʼet dʼeklʌ`rʼirʊjemyh tʌ`vʌrʌf]

489. Have you got any foreign money? - У вас есть иност`ранная ва`люта? [ʊ vʌs jestʼ inʌst`rʌnʌjʌ vʌ`lʼʊtʌ] See Finances

490. I have only personal belongings - У ме`ня `только `личные `вещи [ʊ mʼe`nʼʌ `tɒlʼkʌ `lʼiʧnyje `veʃʼi]

491. These are presents - `Это по`дарки [`etʌ pʌ`dʌrkʼi]

492. I'd like to phone the embassy – Я хо`чу позво`нить в по`сольство [jʌ hʌ`tʃʼʊ pʌzvʌ`nʼitʼ v pʌ`sɒlʼstvʌ]

493. May I go? – `Можно ид`ти? [`mɒʒnʌ i`tʼi]

494. Everything is alright. You may pass on – Всё в по`рядке. `Можете прохо`дить [fsʼe v pʌ`rʼʌtkʼe `mɒʒetʼe prʌhʌ`dʼitʼ]

495. Could you help me with my baggage – Помо`гите мне, по`жалуйста, с бага`жом [pʌmʌ`gʼitʼe mnʼe pʌ`ʒʌlʊstʌ s bʌgʌ`ʒɒm]

496. Can you help me to get a taxi? – Помо`гите мне, по`жалуйста, `вызвать так`си? [pʌmʌ`gʼitʼe mnʼe pʌ`ʒʌlʊstʌ `vyzvʌtʼ tʌk`sʼi]

497. I have lost my ticket / boarding pass / passport / carry-on luggage. Я поте`рял (masculine) / поте`ряла (feminine) би`лет / по`садочный та`лон / `паспорт / руч`ную кладь [jʌ pʌtʼe`rʼʌl / pʌtʼe`rʼʌlʌ bʼi`lʼet / pʌsʌdɒtʃ`nyj tʌ`lɒn / `pʌspɒrt / rʊtʃ`nʊjʊ klʌdʼ]

498. I have lost my child – У ме`ня поте`рялся ре`бёнок [ʊ mʼe`nʼʌ pʌtʼe`rʼʌlsʼʌ rʼe`bʼɒnʌk]

499. I have lost my group – Я отс`тал (masculine) / отс`тала (feminine) от г`руппы [jʌ ʌts`tʌl / ʌts`tʌlʌ ʌt `grʊpy]

500. The flight has been delayed – Рейс за`держивается [rejs zʌ`dʼerʒʼivʌjetsʌ]

501. The flight has been cancelled – Рейс отме`нён [rejs ʌtmʼe`nʼɒn]

502. The flight has arrived in time – Рейс п`рибыл `вовремя [rejs p`rʼibyl `vɒvrʼemʼʌ]

5.2. Around the City

503. Have you got a map? - **У вас есть `карта?** [υ vʌs jest' `kʌrtʌ]

504. I have got a map - **У ме`ня есть `карта** [υ m'e`n'ʌ jest' `kʌrtʌ]

505. Show me on the map please - **Пока`жите, по`жалуйста, на `карте** [pʌkʌ`ʒit'e pʌ`ʒʌlυstʌ nʌ `kʌrte]

506. Show me where we are on the map please - **Пока`жите, по`жалуйста, на `карте, где мы на`ходимся** [pʌkʌ`ʒit'e pʌ`ʒʌlυstʌ nʌ kʌrt'e gd'e my nʌ`hɒd'ims'ʌ]

507. Where am I? - **Где я?** [gd'e jʌ]

508. Help me please, I got lost - **Помо`гите, по`жалуйста, я поте`рялся** (masculine) / **поте`рялась** (feminine) [pʌmʌ`g'it'e pʌ`ʒʌlυstʌ jʌ pʌt'e`r'ʌls'ʌ / pʌt'e`r'ʌlʌs']

509. What is the name of this street? - **Как назы`вается `эта `улица?** [kʌk nʌzy`vʌjetsʌ `etʌ `υl'itsʌ]

510. What is the name of this place? - **Как назы`вается `это `место?** [kʌk nʌzy`vʌjetsʌ `etʌ `m'estʌ]

511. What district is this? - **Какой `это ра`йон?** [kʌ`kɒj `etʌ rʌ`jɒn]

512. Here [place] - **Здесь** [zd'es']

513. Here [direction] - **Сюда** [s'υ`dʌ]

514. Come here - **И`дите сю`да** [ɪ`d'it'e s'υ`d'ʌ]

515. There [place] - **Там** [tʌm]

516. There [direction] - **Ту`да** [tυ`dʌ]

517. Go there - **И`дите ту`да** [ɪ`d'it'e tυ`dʌ]

518. Is it far from here? – `Это да`леко от`сюда? [`etʌ dʌl'e`kɒ ʌt`s'ʊdʌ]

519. It is far from here – `Это недале`ко от`сюда [`etʌ n'edʌl'e`kɒ ʌt`s'ʊdʌ]

520. It is very near – `Это `очень б`лизко [`etʌ `ɒtʃ'en' b`l'iskʌ]

521. Can I walk there from here? – `Можно дой`ти ту`да пеш`ком? [`mɒʤnʌ dʌj`t'i tʊ`dʌ p'eʃ`kɒm]

522. You will need to go by bus / tram / trolleybus / subway – Вам `нужно `ехать на ав`тобусе / трам`вае / трол`лейбусе / мет`ро [vʌm `nʊʒnʌ `jehʌt' nʌ ʌv`tɒbʊs'e / trʌm`vʌje / trʌ`lejbʊs'e / m'et`rɒ]

523. Near this place ... – `Рядом с `этим `местом ... [`r'ʌdʌm s `et'im m'estʌm]

524. Go ... meters / blocks – Прой`дите ... [prʌj`d'it'e ...]

- After any numeral ending with 1 – except 11 – метр / квар`тал [m'etr / kvʌr`tʌl]

- After any numeral ending with 2, 3, 4 – except 12, 13, 14 – `метра / квар`тала [`m'etrʌ / kvʌr`tʌlʌ]

- Nouns after the numerals 11-14 or any numeral ending with 0, 5, 6, 7, 8, 9 – `метров / квар`талов [`m'etrʌf / kvʌr`tʌlʌf]

See Numerals

525. Go straight – И`дите п`рямо [ɪ`d'it'e `pr'ʌmʌ]

526. Cross the road – Перей`дите до`рогу [p'er'ej`d'it'e dʌ`rɒgʊ]

527. Cross the bridge – Перей`дите мост [p'er'ej`d'it'e mɒst]

528. Do not turn anywhere - Ниг`де не сво`рачивайте [n'ig`d'e n'e svʌ`rʌtʃ'ivʌjt'e]

529. Turn left - Повер`ните на`лево [pʌv'er`n'it'e nʌ`l'evʌ]

530. Turn right - Повер`ните нап`раво [pʌv'er`n'it'e nʌp`rʌvʌ]

531. At the traffic light - На свето`форе [nʌ sv'etʌ`fɒr'e]

532. At the crossroad - На перек`рёстке [nʌ p'er'ek`rɒstk'e]

533. To the north - На `север [nʌ `s'ev'er]

534. To the south - На юг [nʌ juk]

535. To the west - На `запад [nʌ `zʌpʌt]

536. To the east - На вос`ток [nʌ vʌs`tɒk]

537. Go up the street - Прой`дите по `улице [prʌj`d'it'e pʌ `ʋl'itse]

538. This is the bedroom community - `Это с`пальный ра`йон [`etʌ s`pʌl'nyj rʌ`jɒn]

539. This is the city center - `Это центр [`etʌ tsentr]

540. I need to get to the city center - Мне `нужно по`пасть в центр [mn'e `nʋʒnʌ pʌ`pʌst' v tsentr]

541. This is the suburb - `Это п`ригород ['etʌ pr'igʌrʌd]

542. There will be a / an ... opposite you - Нап`ротив вас `будет ... [nʌp`rɒt'if vʌs `bʋd'et]

543. There will be a / an ... in front of you - `Перед `вами `будет ... [`p'er'et `vʌmi `bʋd'et ...]

544. There will be a / an ... behind you - Поза`ди вас `будет ... [pʌzʌ`d'i vʌs `bʋd'et ...]

545. There will be a / an ... to your left - С`лева от вас `будет... [s`l′evʌ ʌt vʌs `bʊd′et...]

546. There will be a / an ... to your right - Сп`рава от вас `будет ... [sp`rʌvʌ ʌt vʌs `bʊd′et ...]

547. ... Building - З`дание [`zdʌn′ije]

See Colours

548. ... Big / Small building - Боль`шое / `маленькое з`дание [bʌl′`ʃɒje / `mʌl′en′kʌje `zdʌn′ije]

549. ... High / Low building - Вы`сокое / `низкое з`дание [vy`sɒkʌje / `niskʌje `zdʌn′ije]

550. ... Modern / Ancient building - Совре`менное / ста`ринное з`дание [sʌvr′e`m′enʌje / stʌ`r′inʌje `zdʌn′ije]

551. How many stories are there? - С`колько там эта`жей? [s`kɒl′kʌ tʌm etʌ`ʒej]

552. There are ... stories in the building - В з`дании ... [v z`dʌn′ii]

- After any numeral ending with 1 - except 11 - этаж [e`tʌʒ]

- After any numeral ending with 2, 3, 4 - except 12, 13, 14 - эта`жа [etʌ`ʒʌ]

- After the numerals 11-14 or any numeral ending with 0, 5, 6, 7, 8, 9 - эта`жей [etʌ`ʒej]

See Numerals

553. You'll see a / an ... - Вы у`видите ... [vy ʊ`v′id′it′e ...]

554. ... Block of flats - Многоквар`тирный дом [mnʌgʌkvʌr`t′irnyj dɒm]

555. ... Fountain - Фон`тан [fʌn`tʌn]

556. ... Monument - `Памятник []

557. ... Park - Парк [`pʌm'ʌtn'ik]

558. ... Pedestrian overpass - Над`земный пере`ход [nʌd`z'emnyj p'er'e`hɒd]

559. ... Pedestrian underpass - Под`земный пере`ход [pʌd`z'emnyj p'er'e`hɒd]

560. ... Skyscraper - Небоск`рёб [n'ebʌsk`rɒp]

561. I am looking for a / an ... - Я и`щу ... [jʌ i`ʃ'ʊ ...]

562. ... Alley - Пере`улок [p'er'e`ʊlʌk]

563. ... ATM - Банко`мат [bʌnkʌ`mʌt]

564. ... Cathedral - Со`бор [sʌ`bɒr]

565. ... Circus - Цирк [tsyrk]

566. ... Corner - `Угол [`ʊgʌl]

567. ... Gallery - Гале`рею [gʌl'e`r'ejʊ]

568. ... Museum - Му`зей [mʊ`z'ej]

569. ... Nightclub - Ноч`ной клуб [nʌtʃ`nɒj klʊb]

570. ... Avenue - Прос`пект [prʌs`p'ekt]

571. ... Road - До`рогу [dʌ`rɒgʊ]

572. ... Square - П`лощадь [p`lɒʃ'ʌd']

573. ... Shop - Мага`зин [mʌgʌ`z'in]

See Shops

574. ... Stadium - Стади`он [stʌdi`ɒn]

575. ... Street - `Улицу [`ʊl'itsʊ]

576. ... Theater - Те`атр [t'e`ʌtr]

577. ... Zoo - Зоо`парк [zʌʌ`pʌrk]

578. Excuse me, do you know where ... is situated? – **Изви`ните, вы не з`наете, где на`ходится ...?** [ɪzv'i`n'it'e vy n'e z`nʌjete gd'e nʌ`hɒd'itsʌ ...]

579. ... Amusement park – **Парк развле`чений** [pʌrk rʌzvletʃenij]

580. ... Bank – **Банк** [bʌnk]

581. ... Café – **Ка`фе** [kʌ`fe]

582. ... Church – **`Церковь** [`tserkʌf']

583. ... Cinema – **Кинотеа`тр** [k'inʌt'e`ʌtr]

584. ... Coffee shop – **Ко`фейня** [kʌ`f'ejn'ʌ]

585. ... Department store – **Универ`маг** [ʊn'iv'er`mʌg]

586. ... Grocery – **Продук`товый мага`зин** [prʌdʊk`tɒvyj mʌgʌz'in]

587. ... Market – **`Рынок** [`rynʌk]

588. ... Hospital – **Боль`ница** [bʌl'`n'itsʌ]

589. ... Hostel – **`Хостел** [`hɒstel]

590. ... Hotel – **О`тель** [ʌ`tel']

591. ... Pharmacy – **Ап`тека** [ʌp`t'ekʌ]

592. ... Pizzeria – **Пиц`церия** [p'its`tser'ijʌ]

593. ... Police station – **Отде`ление по`лиции** [ʌd'e`l'en'ije pʌ`litsii]

594. ... Post office – **Поч`та** [`pɒtʃtʌ]

595. ... Restaurant – **Ресто`ран** [r'estʌ`rʌn]

596. ... Shopping center – **Тор`говый центр** [tʌr`gɒvyj tsentr]

597. ... Supermarket – **Супер`маркет** [sʊp'er`mʌrk'et]

598. ... Tourist information office - **Информаци`онный центр для ту`ристов** [ˈɪnfʌrmʌtsˈiˋɒnyj tsentr dlʼʌ tʊˋrʼistʌf]

599. ... Waterpark - **Аква`парк** [ʌkvʌˋpʌrk]

600. Excuse me, do you know how to get to the ...? - **Изви`ните, вы не знаете, как доб`раться до...?** [ˈɪzvʼiˋnʼitʼe, vy nʼe zˋnʌjetʼe kʌk dʌbˋrʌtsʌ dɒ...]

601. ... Airport - **Аэропор`та** [ʌerʌpʌrˋtʌ]

602. ... Bus stop - **Ав`тобусой оста`новки** [ʌfˋtɒbʊsɒj ʌstʌˋnɒfkʼi]

603. ... Railway station - **Вок`зала** [ʊʌkˋzʌlʌ]

604. ... Subway station - **С`танции мет`ро** [sˋtʌntsii mʼetˋrɒ]

605. ... Tram stop - **Трам`вайной оста`новки** [trʌmˋvʌjnʌj ʌstʌˋnɒfkʼi]

606. ... Trolleybus stop - **Трол`лейбусной оста`новки** [trʌˋlʼejbʊsnʌj ʌstʌˋnɒfkʼi]

5.2. Trains

607. You need to go by train - **Вам `нужно `ехать на `поезде** [vʌm ˋnʊʒnʌ jehʌtʼ nʌ ˋpɒjezdʼe]

608. You need an electric suburban train - **Вам `нужно ехать на электричке** [vʌm ˋnʊʒnʌ jehʌtʼ nʌ elʼekˋtrʼitʃkʌ]

(Note that there is a special type of train in Russia called: электричка [el'ek`tr'itʃkʌ] - it is a suburban electric train which has only sitting accommodation and goes between a city and its suburbs and nearby towns. The more general term поезд [`pɒjezd'] - train - is usually used for long-distance trains going between various big cities. You can buy tickets for both long-distance trains and suburban electric trains at railway stations. If you want a ticket for a suburban electric train, you buy it without a reserved seat number and just sit wherever you want.)

609. How can I get to the railway station? - Как доб`раться до железнодо`рожного вок`зала? [Kʌk dʌb`rʌtsʌ dʌ ʒel'eznʌdʌ`rɒʒnʌvʌ vʌk`zʌlʌ?]

610. Where is the railway ticket office? - Где на`ходится железнодо`рожная `касса? [gd'e nʌ`hɒd'itsʌ ʒel'eznʌdʌ`rɒʒnʌjʌ `kʌsʌ]

611. How much is the ticket to …? - `Сколько с`тоит би`лет до …? [s`kɒl'kʌ s`tɒit b'i`l'et dʌ …]

612. I need a ticket to … - Мне `нужен би`лет до … [mn'e `nuʒen b'i`l'et dʌ …]

613. I need a one-way ticket - Мне `нужен би`лет в о`дин ко`нец [mn'e `nuʒen b'i`l'et v ʌ`d'in kʌ`n'ets]

614. I need a return ticket - Мне `нужен об`ратный би`лет [mn'e `nuʒen ʌb`rʌtnyj b'i`l'et]

615. From what platform does the electric suburban train to … leave? - С ка`кой плат`формы отправ`ляется элект`ричка до с`танции …? [s kʌ`kɒj plʌt`fɒrmy ʌtprʌv`l'ʌjetsʌ el'ekt`r'itʃkʌ dʌ s`tʌntsii …]

616. The electric suburban train to … leaves at platform … - Элект`ричка до с`танции … отправ`ляется с

65

плат`формы ... [el'ekt`r'itʃkʌ dʌ s`tʌntsii ... ʌtprʌv`l'ʌjetsʌ s plʌt`fɒrmy ...]

617. Could you tell me where the platform ... is? – **Скажите, по`жалуйста, где плат`форма ...?** [skʌ`ʒ'it'e pʌ`ʒʌlʊstʌ gd'e plʌt`fɒrmʌ ...]

See Numerals

618. What stop is it now – do you know? – **Вы з`наете, ка`кая сей`час оста`новка?** [ʋy z`nʌjet'e kʌ`kʌjʌ sej`tʃʌs ʌstʌ`nɒfkʌ]

619. What side of the carriage is the exit at the next stop going to be – do you know? – **Вы з`наете, с ка`кой сторо`ны `будет `выход на с`ледующей оста`новке?** [ʋy z`nʌjete s kʌ`kɒj stʌrʌ`ny `bʊd'et `vyhɒd nʌ sl'edʊjʊʃ'ej ʌstʌ`nɒfke]

620. How long is it to the station ...? – **С`колько `ехать до с`танции ...?** [s`kɒl'kʌ jehʌt' dʌ s`tʌntsii ...]

(Note that if you buy a ticket for a long-distance train, there are usually several types of accommodation available:

Си`дячий ва`гон [s'i`d'ʌtʃ'ij vʌ`gɒn] – sitting carriage, the cheapest type of railway accommodation where you have only a seat, even for an overnight journey.

**Плац`карт** [plʌts`kʌrt] – economy class sleeping car, it is an open-type carriage where there are 54 bunks, arranged in open compartments of two lower-level bunks and two upper-level bunks and a table on one side of one lower-level bunk and one upper-level bunk, with an aisle between the two sides; there are no doors in this kind of carriage so there is no privacy and it is rather noisy; if you travel by this type of carriage, it is advisable to avoid places 34-38, which are situated close to the toilets and thus are the noisiest ones.

**Ку`пе** [kʊ`pe] – first class sleeping car with nine separate compartments with two lower-level bunks and two upper-level bunks each, a fold-down table and a sliding door.

СВ [es ve] – luxurious sleeping car with nine separate compartments with only two lower-level bunks and a folding table.

In all types of sleeping cars, you can usually buy tea and some snacks from the railroad conductor. The toilets are situated at the ends of each carriage. There is bedlinen provided in the first class and luxury sleeping cars, as for the economy class sleeping cars, you sometimes have to pay separately for it.

To buy a ticket or get on board of a long-distance train, you will need to show your ID, e.g. your passport.)

621. Show me your ID, please – **Пока`жите, по`жалуйста, `паспорт** [pʌkʌ`ʒi'te pʌ`ʒalʊstʌ `pʌspʌrt]

622. I need a place in a sitting carriage – **Мне `нужно `место в си`дячем ва`гоне** [mn'e `nʊʒnʌ `m'estʌ v s'id'ʌtʃ'em vʌ`gɒn'e]

623. I need a place in an economy class sleeping car – **Мне `нужен плац`карт** [mn'e `nʊʒen plʌts`kʌrt]

624. I need a place in a first-class sleeping car – **Мне `нужно ку`пе** [mn'e `nʊʒnʌ kʊ`pe]

625. I need a place in a luxurious sleeping car – **Мне `нужно СВ** [mn'e `nʊʒnʌ es ve]

626. I would like a lower-level bunk – **`Можно мне `нижнюю `полку?** [`mɒʒnʌ mn'e `n'iʒnʊjʊ `pɒlkʊ]

627. I would like an upper level bunk – **`Можно мне `верхнюю `полку?** [`mɒʒnʌ mn'e `verhnʊjʊ `pɒlkʊ]

628. No tickets available – **Би`летов нет** [b'i`l'etʌf n'et]

629. I need a ticket for <the date> – Мне `нужен би`лет на … [mnʲe `nuʒen bʲiˈlʲet nʌ …]

See **Numerals** and **Dates**

630. What time does the train to … leave? – Ког`да отправ`ляется `поезд до с`танции …? [kʌgˈdʌ ʌtprʌvˈlʲajetsʌ `pɒeʃt dʌ sˈtʌntsii …]

631. What time does the train to … arrive? – Ког`да прибы`вает `поезд до с`танции …? [kʌgˈdʌ prʲibyˈvʌjet 'pɒjest dʌ sˈtʌntsii …]

632. From what platform does the train number … to … leave? – С ка`кой плат`формы отправ`ляется `поезд `номер … до с`танции …? [s kʌˈkɒj plʌtˈfɒrmy ʌtprʌvˈlʲajetsʌ 'pɒjest ˈnɒmʲer … dʌ sˈtʌntsii …]

See **Numerals**

633. The train number … to … leaves at platform … – `Поезд `номер … до с`танции … отправ`ляется с плат`формы … [ˈpɒjest ˈnɒmʲer … dʌ sˈtʌntsii … ʌtprʌvˈlʲajetsʌ s plʌtˈfɒrmy …]

See **Numerals**

634. How long is this train stop? – С`колько прод`лится `эта оста`новка? [sˈkɒlʲkʌ prʌdˈlʲitsʌ ˈetʌ ʌstʌˈnɒfkʌ]

635. Please wake me up an hour before the train arrives – Разбу`дите ме`ня, по`жалуйста, за час до при`бытия [rʌzbuˈdʲitʲe mʲeˈnʲʌ pʌˈʒʌlustʌ zʌ tʃʌs dʌ prʲiˈbytʲijʌ]

636. I need some hot water – Мне нуж`на го`рячая во`да [mnʲe nuʒˈnʌ gʌˈrʲʌtʃʌjʌ vʌˈdʌ]

637. I want to buy some tea – Я хо`чу ку`пить чай [jʌ hʌˈtʃʲu kuˈpʲitʲ tʃʌj]

638. I need the bedlinen – is it free? – **Мне `нужно пос`тельное бе`льё. `Это бесп`латно?** [mn'e `nuznʌ pʌs`t'el'nʌje beljɒ 'etʌ b'esp`lʌtnʌ]

639. How much is the bedlinen? – **С`колько с`тоит пос`тельное бе`льё?** [s`kɒl'kʌ s`tɒ'it pʌs`t'el'nʌje b'e`ljɒ]

640. Are you the train conductor? – **Вы провод`ник?** [ʋy prʌʋʌd`n'ik]

641. Show me please where the toilet is – **Пока`жите, по`жалуйста, где туа`лет** [pʌkʌ`ʒ'it'e pʌ`ʒʌlʊstʌ gd'e tʊʌ`l'et]

642. Where is the diner carriage? – **Где на`ходится ва`гон-ресто`ран?** [gd'e nʌ`hɒd'itsʌ ʋʌ`gɒn-r'estʌ`rʌn]

643. The diner carriage is in carriage number ... – **Ва`гон-ресто`ран распо`ложен в ва`гоне `номер ...** [ʋʌ`gɒn-r'estʌ`rʌn rʌspʌ`lɒʒen v ʋʌ`gɒn'e `nɒm'er ...]

See Numerals

644. Could you close the door to the compartment please? – **Зак`ройте, по`жалуйста, дверь в ку`пе** [zʌk`rɒjt'e pʌ`ʒʌlʊstʌ dv'er' v kʊ`pe]

645. Could you tell me where the electric socket is please? – **Ска`жите, по`жалуйста, где ро`зетка?** [skʌʒ'it'e pʌ`ʒʌlʊstʌ gd'e rʌ`z'etkʌ]

646. Could you turn on the lights please? – **Вклю`чите, по`жалуйста, свет?** [vklʊ`tʃ'it'e pʌ`ʒʌlʊstʌ sv'et]

647. Could you turn off the lights please? – **`Выключите, по`жалуйста, свет?** [`ʋyklʊtʃ'it'e pʌ`ʒʌlʊstʌ sv'et]

648. Do not make noise please – **Не шу`мите, по`жалуйста** [n'e ʃʊ`m'it'e pʌ`ʒʌlʊstʌ]

649. Have we already arrived? – Мы у`же при`ехали? [my ʊ`ʒe pr′i`jehʌl′i]

5.4. Public Transport

650. You need to go by bus – Вам `нужно `ехать на ав`тобусе [vʌm `nuʒnʌ jehʌt′ nʌ ʌf`tɒbʊs′e]

651. You need to go by tram – Вам `нужно `ехать на трам`вае [vʌm `nuʒnʌ jehʌt′ nʌ trʌm`vʌje]

652. You need to go by trolleybus – Вам `нужно ехать на трол`лейбусе [vʌm `nuʒnʌ jehʌt′ nʌ trʌ`lejbʊs′e]

653. You will need a bus / tram / trolleybus number ... – Са`дитесь на ав`тобус / трам`вай / трол`лейбус но`мер ... [sʌ`d′it′es′ nʌ ʌf`tɒbʊs / trʌm`vʌj / trʌ`l′ejbʊs `nɒm′er ...]

654. Where does the bus / tram / trolleybus number ... stop? – Где оста`навливается ав`тобус / трам`вай / трол`лейбус `номер ...? [gd′e ʌstʌ`nʌvl′ivʌjetsʌ ʌf`tɒbʊs / trʌ`mvʌj / trʌ`l′ejbʊs `nɒm′er ...]

See Numerals

655. Am I going to reach ... if I go with you? – Я до`еду до с`танции ...? [jʌ dʌ`jedʊ dʌ s`tʌntsii ...]

656. When does the next / last bus leave? – Ког`да у`ходит с`ледующий / пос`ледний ав`тобус? [kʌg`dʌ ʊ`hɒd′it s`l′edʊjʊʃ′ij / pʌs`l′edn′ij ʌf`tɒbʊs]

657. Is this the conductor? – `Это кон`дуктор? [′etʌ kʌn`dʊktʌr]

658. You need to change to the bus / tram / trolleybus number ... – Вам `нужно пере`сесть на ав`тобус / трам`вай / трол`лейбус `номер ... [vʌm `nuʒnʌ p′er′e`s′est′ nʌ ʌf`tɒbʊs / trʌm`vʌj / trʌ`l′ejbʊs `nɒm′er ...]

See Numerals

659. Which bus / tram / trolleybus goes to the center ...? – Ка`кой ав`тобус и`дёт в центр? [kʌ`kɒj ʌf`tɒbʊs 'i`d'ɒt v tsentr]

660. I need to reach the place called ... – Мне `нужно доб`раться до ... [mn'e `nʊʒnʌ dʌb`rʌt'sʌ dʌ ...]

661. Is there a schedule? – Есть распи`сание? [jest' rʌsp'i`sʌn'ije]

662. Where is the schedule? – Где распи`сание? [gd'e rʌsp'i`sʌn'ije]

663. Look at the schedule – Посмот`рите в распи`сание [pʌsmʌt`r'it'e v rʌsp'i`sʌn'ije]

664. What is the fare? – С`колько с`тоит про`езд? [s'kɒl'kʌ s`tɒ'it prʌ`jest]

665. I need to buy ... tickets – Мне `нужно ку`пить ... [mn'e `nʊʒnʌ kʊ`p'it']

 - After any numeral ending with 1 – except 11 – би`лет [b'i`l'et]

 - After any numeral ending with 2, 3, 4 – except 12, 13, 14 – би`лета [b'i`l'etʌ]

 - After the numerals 11-14 or any numeral ending with 0, 5, 6, 7, 8, 9 – би`летов [b'il'etʌf]

See Numerals

666. Can I pay by card? – `Можно опла`тить `картой? [`mɒʒnʌ ʌplʌ`t'it' `kʌrtʌj]

667. I have no change, sorry – Изви`ните, у ме`ня нет с`дачи ['ızv`n'it'e ʊ m'e`n'ʌ n'et s`dʌtʃ'i]

668. Here is my ticket – Вот мой би`лет [vɒt mɒj b'i`l'et]

669. Sit down, please – Са`дитесь, по`жалуйста [sʌ`d'it'es' pʌ`ʒʌlʊstʌ]

670. Excuse me, may I pass? – `Можно прой`ти? [`mɒʒnʌ prʌj`t'i]

671. Excuse me, let me pass please – Пропус`тите ме`ня, по`жалуйста [prʌpʊs`t'it'e m'e`n'ʌ pʌ`ʒʌlʊstʌ]

672. Are you getting out at the next stop? – Вы вы`ходите на с`ледующей оста`новке? [vy vy`hɒd'it'e nʌ s`l'edʊjʊʃ'ej ʌstʌ`nɒfk'e]

673. I am getting out at the next stop – Я выхо`жу на с`ледующей оста`новке [jʌ vyhʌ`ʒʊ nʌ s`l'edʊjʊʃ'ej ʌstʌ`nɒfk'e]

674. You need to catch a share-taxi number – Вам нуж`на маршрутка номер ... (Note that there is a specific kind of transport typical for Russian cities – марш`рутка [mʌrʃ`rʊtkʌ]; it is a small bus, a kind of shared taxi owned by a privately owned public transport company; unlike buses, trams, and trolleys, which stop at established stops whether a passenger makes any signals or not, марш`рутка usually does not have any regular stops – you should *tell* the driver where you want to get out.)

675. Stop here please – Остано`вите, по`жалуйста, здесь [ʌstʌnʌ`v'it'e pʌ`ʒʌlʊstʌ zd'es']

676. I need to get out here – Мне `нужно `выйти здесь [mn'e `nʊʒnʌ `vyjt'i zd'es']

677. Stop at the next bus stop please – Остано`вите, по`жалуйста, на с`ледующей ав`тобусной оста`новке [ʌstʌnʌ`v'it'e pʌ`ʒʌlʊstʌ nʌ s`l'edʊjʊʃ'ej ʌf`tɒbʊsnʌj ʌstʌ`nɒfk'e]

678. Stop near that pedestrian crossing please – **Остано`вите, по`жалуйста, у то`го пере`хода** [ʌstʌnʌ`v'it'e pʌ`ʒʌlʊstʌ ʊ tʌ`vʌ p'er'e`hɒdʌ]

679. Stop near that building please – **Остано`вите, по`жалуйста, у того з`дания** [ʌstʌnʌ`v'it'e pʌ`ʒʌlʊstʌ ʊ tʌ`vʌ z`dʌn'ijʌ]

680. You need to use the subway – **Вам `нужно `ехать на мет`ро** [vʌm `nʊʒnʌ jehʌt' nʌ m'et`rɒ]

(Note that depending on a city, there may be different types of subway tickets – e.g. you can buy a token for a one-time ride in Saint-Petersburg or a paper card for a particular number of rides in Moscow; also, there are usually unified passes available, for which you can add some money at any moment, using special ticket machines or the services of a cashier, as well as monthly or yearly passes; one ride does not depend on any zones – you can get in on a subway station and spend however long inside, once you have left the subway you will have to pay again to re-enter it.)

681. I need a unified subway pass – **Мне `нужен е`диный проезд`ной** [mn'e `nʊʒen je`d'inyj prʌjez`nɒj]

682. I need to buy ... rides – **Мне `нужно** ... [mn'e `nʊʒnʌ ...]

- After any numeral ending with 1 – except 11 – **по`ездку** [pʌ`jestkʊ]

- After any numeral ending with 2, 3, 4 – except 12, 13, 14 – **по`ездки** [pʌ`jestk'i]

- After the numerals 11-14 or any numeral ending with 0, 5, 6, 7, 8, 9 – **по`ездок** [pʌ`jezdʌk]

See Numerals

683. I need to buy ... tokens – **Мне `нужно** ... [mn'e `nʊʒnʌ ...]

- After any numeral ending with 1 - except 11 - же`тон [ʒe`tʌn]

- After any numeral ending with 2, 3, 4 - except 12, 13, 14 - же`тона [ʒe`tʌnʌ]

- After the numerals 11-14 or any numeral ending with 0, 5, 6, 7, 8, 9 - же`тонов [ʒe`tʌnʌf]

See Numerals

684. The next station is ... - С`ледующая оста`новка ... [s`l'edujuʃ'ʌjʌ ʌstʌ`nɒfkʌ ...]

685. You can change at the station ... - Пере`ход на с`танцию ... [p'er'e`hɒd nʌ s`tʌnts'iju ...]

686. Mind the doors - Осто`рожно, д`вери закры`ваются [ʌstʌ`rɒʒnʌ d`v'er'i zʌkry`vʌjutsʌ]

687. Do not run on the escalators - Не `бегайте по эска`латору [n'e `b'egʌjt'e pʌ eskʌ`lʌtʌru]

5.5. Cars

688. Could you give me a lift to ...? - `Можете подвез`ти ме`ня до ...? [`mɒʒet'e m'e`n'ʌ pʌdv'es`t'i dʌ ...]

689. You need to catch a taxi - Вам `нужно пой`мать так`си [vʌm `nuʒnʌ pʌj`mʌt' tʌk`s'i]

690. Can you call me a taxi please? - `Вызовите мне, по`жалуйста, так`си [`vyzʌv'it'e mn'e pʌ`ʒalustʌ tʌk`s'i]

691. You need to go by car - Вам `нужно `ехать на ма`шине [vʌm `nuʒnʌ `jehʌt' nʌ mʌ`ʃin'e]

692. I want to rent a car - Я хо`чу в`зять в а`ренду ма`шину [jʌ hʌ`tʃ'u v`z'ʌt' v ʌ`r'endu mʌ`ʃinu]

693. I can drive a car - Я у`мею во`дить ма`шину [jʌ u`m'eju vʌ`d'it' mʌ`ʃinu]

694. Here is my driving license – **Вот мо`и во`дительские пра`ва** [ʊɒt mʌ`i vʌ`d'it'el'sk'ije prʌ`vʌ]

695. Do I need to buy any insurance? – **Мне `нужно поку`пать стра`ховку?** [mn'e `nuʒnʌ pʌkʊ`pʌt' strʌ`hɒfkʊ]

696. How much does the insurance cost? – **С`колько с`тоит стра`ховка?** [s`kɒl'kʌ s`tɒ'it strʌ`hɒfkʌ]

697. How much does this insurance cover? – **С`колько покры`вает эта стра`ховка?** [s`kɒl'kʌ pʌkry`vʌjet `etʌ strʌ`hɒfkʌ]

698. Where do I need to return the car? – **Где `именно `нужно вер`нуть ма`шину?** [gd'e `im'enʌ `nuʒnʌ v'er`nʊt' mʌ`ʃinʊ]

699. When do I need to return the car? – **Ког`да `именно `нужно вер`нуть ма`шину?** [kʌg`dʌ `im'enʌ `nuʒnʌ v'er`nʊt' mʌ`ʃinʊ]

700. Do you want an automatic or manual gearbox? – **Вы хо`тите ма`шину с автома`тической или руч`ной ко`робкой пере`дач?** [vy hʌ`t'it'e mʌ`ʃinʊ s ʌvtʌmʌ`t'itʃ'eskaj il'i rʊtʃ`nɒj kʌ`rɒbkʌj p'er'edʌtʃ]

701. I will take an automatic gearbox – **Я возь`му ма`шину с автома`тической ко`робкой пере`дач** [jʌ vʌz`mʊ mʌ`ʃinʊ s ʌvtʌmʌ`t'itʃ'eskaj kʌ`rɒbkʌj p'er'edʌtʃ]

702. I will take a manual gearbox – **Я возь`му ма`шину с руч`ной ко`робкой пере`дач** [jʌ vʌz`mʊ mʌ`ʃinʊ s rʊtʃ`nɒj kʌ`rɒbkʌj p'er'edʌtʃ]

703. I will take this car – **Я возь`му вот `эту ма`шину** [jʌ vʌz`mʊ `etʊ mʌ`ʃinʊ]

704. What type of fuel does this car consume? - **Ка`кой тип `топлива потреб`ляет `эта ма`шина?** [kʌ`kɒj t'ip `tɒpl'ivʌ pʌtr'eb`l'ʌjet `etʌ mʌ`ʃinʌ]

705. Diesel - **ДТ / со`лярка** [sʌ`l'ʌrkʌ]

706. 92 RON - **АИ-92 / девя`носто-вто`рой бен`зин** [d'ev'ʌ`nɒstʌ vtʌ`rɒj b'en`z'in]

707. 95 RON - **АИ-95 / девя`носто-`пятый бен`зин** [d'ev'ʌ`nɒstʌ `p'ʌtyj b'en`z'in]

708. 98 RON - **АИ-98 / девя`носто-вось`мой бен`зин** [d'ev'ʌ`nɒstʌ vʌs"mɒjb'en`z'in]

709. How much does the rent cost per day / per week? - **С`колько с`тоит а`ренда в день / в `месяц?** [s`kɒl'kʌ s`tɒ'it ʌ`r'endʌ v den' / v `m'es'ʌts]

710. Here is your contract - **Вот ваш дого`вор** [vɒt vʌʃ dʌgʌ`vɒr]

711. Where is a petrol station? - **Где на`ходится зап`равка?** [gd'e nʌ`hɒd'itsʌ zʌp`rʌfkʌ]

712. I need to fill up the fuel tank - **Мне `нужно зап`равить ма`шину** [mn'e `nuʒnʌ zʌp`rʌv'it' mʌ`ʃinu]

713. I need ... liters of petrol / diesel - **Мне `нужно ...** [mn'e `nuʒnʌ]

- After any numeral ending with 1 - except 11 - **литр бен`зина / `дизеля** [l'itr b'en`z'inʌ / `d'iz'el'ʌ]

- After any numeral ending with 2, 3, 4 - except 12, 13, 14 - **`литра бен`зина / `дизеля** [`l'itrʌ b'en`z'inʌ / `d'iz'el'ʌ]

- After the numerals 11-14 or any numeral ending with 0, 5, 6, 7, 8, 9 - **`литров бен`зина / `дизеля** [`l'itrʌf b'en`z'inʌ / `d'iz'el'ʌ]

See **Numerals** and **Measurements**

714. Thank you, I do not need any help with my car - **Спа`сибо, мне не нуж`на `помощь с ма`шиной** [spʌs'ibʌ mn'e n'e nuʒ`nʌ `pɒmʌʃ' s mʌ`ʃ'inʌj]

715. Could you please help me to fill up the fuel tank? - **Помо`гите мне, по`жалуйста, зап`равиться?** [pʌmʌ`g'it'e mn'e pʌ`ʒʌlustʌ zʌp`rʌv'itsʌ]

716. Where do I have to pay for the petrol? - **Где пла`тить за бен`зин?** [gd'e plʌ`t'it' zʌ b'en`z'in]

717. My petrol pump number is ... - **У ме`ня ко`лонка `номер ...** [u m'e`n'ʌ kʌ`lɒnkʌ `nɒm'er]

See **Numerals**

718. I need to wash the car - **Мне `нужно по`мыть ма`шину** [mn'e `nuʒnʌ pʌ`myt' mʌ`ʃinu]

719. Where is the nearest car wash? - **Где бли`жайшая авто`мойка?** [gd'e bl'i`ʒʌjʃʌjʌ ʌvtʌ`mɒjkʌ]

720. I need some water for the windshield washer - **Мне нуж`на во`да для стеклоомы`вателя** [mn'e nuʒ`nʌ vʌ`dʌ dl'ʌ st'eklʌmy`vʌt'el'ʌ]

721. Could you please wipe my windshield? - **Прот`рите, по`жалуйста, ветро`вое стек`ло** [prʌt`r'it'e pʌ`ʒʌlustʌ v'etrʌ`vɒje st'ek`lɒ]

722. I need a mechanic - **Мне `нужен ме`ханик** [mn'e `nuʒen m'e`hʌn'ik]

723. I need to change the oil - **Мне `нужно поме`нять `масло** [mn'e `nuʒnʌ pʌm'e`n'ʌt' `mʌslʌ]

724. I have a flat tyre - **У ме`ня с`пущена `шина** [u m'e`n'ʌ s`puʃ'enʌ `ʃinʌ]

725. I need to pump up my tyre - **Мне `нужно нака`чать `шину** [mn'e `nuʒnʌ nʌkʌ`tʃʌt' `ʃinu]

726. My tyre seems to have been damaged - `Кажется, у ме`ня про`колота `шина [`kʌʒetsʌ ʋ m'e`n'ʌ prʌ`kɒlʌtʌ `ʃinʌ]

727. I need a patch on my tyre - `Нужно с`делать зап`латку на `шине [`nuʒnʌ s`d'elʌt' zʌp`lʌtkʋ nʌ `ʃin'e]

728. How can I call a tow truck? - Как `вызвать эваку`атор? [kʌk mn'e `vyzvʌt' evʌkʋ`ʌtʌr]

729. The engine does not start - Д`вигатель не за`водится [d`v'igʌt'el' n'e zʌ`vɒd'itsʌ]

730. Parking is prohibited - Пар`ковка запреще`на [pʌr`kɒfkʌ zʌpr'eʃ'e`nʌ]

731. What is the speed limit here? - Ка`кой здесь скорост`ной ре`жим? [kʌ`kɒj zd'es' skʌrʌs`nɒj re`ʒim]

732. There are speed cameras - Тут `камеры, прове`ряющие с`корость [tʋt `kʌm'ery prʌv'e`r'ʌjʋʃ'ije s`kɒrʌst']

733. No passage - Про`езд запре`щён [prʌ`jest zʌp`reʃ'en]

734. One-way street - Односто`ронняя `улица [ʌdnʌstʌ`rɒn'ʌjʌ `ʋl'itsʌ]

735. Excuse me, how do I get to the freeway from here? - Ска`жите, по`жалуйста, как доб`раться от`сюда до т`рассы? [skʌ`ʒit'e pʌ`ʒʌlʋstʌ kʌk dʌb`rʌtsʌ ʌts'ʋdʌ dʌ t`rʌsy]

736. Where is a parking lot situated? - Где на`ходится пар`ковка? [gd'e nʌ`hɒd'itsʌ pʌr`kɒfkʌ]

737. This is a paid parking facility - `Это п`латная пар`ковка ['etʌ p`lʌtnʌjʌ pʌr`kɒfkʌ]

738. Where can I pay for the parking? – **Где `можно запла`тить за пар`ковку?** [gd'e `mɒʒnʌ zʌplʌ`t'it' zʌ pʌr`kɒfkʊ]

Chapter 6. Sightseeing and Entertainment

6.1. Sightseeing

739. What places do you recommend for me to visit around here? – **В ка`кие мес`та поб`лизости порекомен`дуете схо`дить?** [v kʌ`k'ije m'es`tʌ pʌb`l'izʌst'i pʌr'ekʌm'en`dujet'e shʌ`d'it']

740. Is it worth visiting ...? – **С`тоит ли посе`щать ...?** [s`tɒ'it l'i pʌs'e`ʃ'ʌt' ...]

741. Do you like ...? – **Вам н`равится ...?** [vʌm n`rʌv'itsʌ ...]

742. Do you like this place? – **Вам н`равится `это `место?** [vʌm n`rʌv'itsʌ 'etʌ `m'estʌ]

743. What museums / galleries / theaters can you recommend for me to go to? – **В ка`кие му`зеи / гале`реи / те`атры посо`ветуете схо`дить?** [v kʌ`k'ije mʊ`z'ei / gʌl'e`r'ei / t'e`ʌtry pʌsʌ`v'etujet'e shʌ`d'it']

744. What is your favorite place around here? – **Ка`кое у вас лю`бимое `место здесь?** [kʌ`kɒe ʊ vʌs l'ʊ`b'imʌje `m'estʌ zd'es']

745. What is your favorite place in this city? – **Ка`кое у вас лю`бимое `место в `городе?** [kʌ`kɒje ʊ vʌs l'ʊ`b'imʌje `m'estʌ v `gɒrʌd'e]

746. What place do you recommend for me to go to relax? – **Ка`кое `место посо`ветуете, ч`тобы расс`лабиться?** [kʌ`kɒje `m'estʌ pʌsʌ`v'etujet'e tʃ`tɒby rʌs`lʌb'itsʌ]

747. What is the most impressive place to visit? – **Где `можно полу`чить незабы`ваемые впечат`ления?**

[gd'e ˋmɒʒnʌ pʌlʊˋtʃ'it' n'ezʌbyˋvʌjemyje vp'etʃʌtl'en'ijʌ]

748. What is the best place to have a walk? – Где ˋлучше всеˋго прогуˋляться? [gd'e ˋlʊtʃ'e vs'eˋvɒ prʌgʊˋl'ʌtsʌ]

749. Where would you go if you came to Russia for the first time? – Куˋда бы вы пошˋли, ˋесли бы ˋпервый раз приˋехали в Росˋсию? [kʊˋdʌ by vy pʌʃˋl'i esl'i by p'ervyj rʌz pr'iˋjehʌl'i v rʌˋs'ijʊ]

750. I would like to see something traditional / modern – Я хоˋчу уˋвидеть что-нибудь традициˋонное / совреˋменное [jʌ hʌˋtʃ'ʊ ʊˋv'id'et' ʃˋtɒn'ibʊd' trʌd'itsiˋɒnʌje / sʌvr'eˋm'enʌje]

751. What is the most popular place around here? – Каˋкое здесь ˋсамое популˋярное ˋместо? [kʌˋkɒje zd'es' ˋsʌmʌje pʌpʊˋl'ʌrnʌje ˋm'estʌ]

752. What place do tourists like most of all? – Каˋкое ˋместо ˋбольше всеˋго нˋравится туˋристам? [kʌˋkɒje ˋm'estʌ ˋbɒl'ʃe vs'eˋvɒ nˋrʌv'itsʌ tʊˋr'istʌm]

753. Is it free? – ˋЭто беспˋлатно? ['etʌ b'espˋlʌtnʌ]

754. How much do I have to pay for the entrance? – Сˋколько ˋнужно заплаˋтить за вход? [sˋkɒl'kʌ ˋnʊʒnʌ zʌplʌˋt'it' zʌ vhɒt]

755. Can you take a photo of me / us? – Вы ˋможете меˋня / нас сфотограˋфировать? [vy ˋmɒʒet'e m'eˋn'ʌ / nʌs sfʌtʌgrʌˋf'irʌvʌt']

756. Tell me about this place, please – Рассказˋжите об ˋэтом ˋместе / зˋдании, поˋжалуйста [rʌskʌˋʒit'e ʌb 'etʌm mest'e / zˋdʌn'ii pʌˋʒʌlʊstʌ]

757. Where can I buy some souvenirs? – Где ˋможно куˋпитьувеˋниры? [gd'e ˋmɒʒnʌ kʊˋp'it' sʊv'eˋn'iry]

758. Where can I go to watch a football / volleyball / basketball match? – Ку`да схо`дить на фут`больный / волей`больный / баскет`больный матч? [kʋ`dʌ `mɔʒnʌ shʌ`d'it' nʌ fʋt`bɒl'nyj / vʌl'ej`bɒl'nyj / bʌsk'et`bɒl'nyj mʌtʃ]

759. Where can I play ...? – Где `можно поиг`рать в ...? [gd'e `mɔʒnʌ pʌig`rʌt' v ...] See Sport

760. Let's play ... – Да`вайте (polite / plural) / Да`вай (informal) поиг`раем в ... [dʌ`vʌjt'e / dʌ`vʌj pʌig`rʌjem v ...]

761. Are there any places to jog nearby? – Где поб`лизости `можно по`бегать? [gd'e pʌb`l'izʌst'i `mɔʒnʌ pʌ`b'egʌt']

762. Is there any place to work out? – Где `можно потрениро`ваться? [gd'e `mɔʒnʌ pʌtr'en'irʌ`vʌtsʌ]

763. What gym do you recommend for me to go to? – В ка`кой трена`жёрный зал посо`ветуете пой`ти? [ʋ kʌ`kɒj tr'enʌ`ʒɒrnyj zʌl pʌsʌ`v'etʋjet'e pʌjt'i]

764. Are there any parks? – Здесь есть `парки? [zd'es' jest' `pʌrk'i]

765. Is there a gaming club around here? – Здесь есть ком`пьютерный клуб?[zd'es' jest' kʌmp`jʋternyj klʋp]

766. I'm going to a bar tonight – Се`годня я пой`ду в бар / ноч`ной клуб [s'e`vɒdn'ʌ jʌ pʌj`dʋ v bʌr / nʌtʃ`nɒj klʋp]

767. Are there any good hookah bars? – Здесь есть хо`рошие ка`льянные? [zd'es' jest' hʌ`rɒʃije kʌl'`jʌnyje]

768. How long will we be there? – С`колько мы там `будем нахо`диться? [s`kɒl'kʌ my tʌm `bʋd'em nʌhʌ`d'itsʌ]

769. Are there any walking tours available? – Здесь есть пеше`ходные `туры?[zd'es' jest' p'eʃe`hɒdnye `tʊry]

770. How long will it take? – С`колько `это зай`мёт в`ремени? [s`kɒl'kʌ 'etʌ zʌj`m'ɒt v`r'em'en'i]

771. What do I need to take with me? – Что `нужно в`зять с со`бой? [ʃtɒ `nʊʒnʌ vz'ʌt' s sʌ`bɒj]

772. Where can I book a general sightseeing tour? – Где `можно зака`зать об`зорную экс`курсию? [gd'e 'mɒnʌ zʌkʌ`zʌt' ʌb`zɒrnʊjʊ eks`kʊrs'ijʊ]

773. How much does the tour cost? – С`колько с`тоит экс`курсия? [s`kɒl'kʌ s`tɒ'it eks`kʊrs'ijʌ]

774. Is it a bus tour? – `Это ав`тобусная экс`курсия? ['etʌ ʌf`tɒbʊsnʌjʌ eks`kʊrs'ijʌ]

775. What kind of tours do you offer? – Ка`кие экс`курсии вы предла`гаете? [kʌ`k'ie eks`kʊrs'ii vy pr'edlʌ`gʌjet'e]

776. What is included in this tour? – Что в`ходит в `эту экс`курсию? [ʃtɒ v`hɒd'it v `etʊ eks`kʊrs'ijʊ]

777. What time does the tour start? – Ког`да начи`нается `эта экс`курсия? [kɒg`dʌ nʌtʃ'i`nʌjetsʌ `etʌ eks`kʊrs'ijʌ]

778. What time does the tour end? – Ког`да за`канчивается `эта экс`курсия? [kʌg`dʌ zʌ`kʌntʃ'ivʌjetsʌ `etʌ eks`kʊrs'ijʌ]

779. I would like to make a reservation – Я хо`чу забро`нировать би`лет [jʌ hʌ`tʃʊ zʌbrʌ`n'irʌvʌt' b'i`l'et]

780. What is on this week? – Ка`кие со`бытия `будут на `этой не`деле? [kʌ`k'ie sʌ`byt'ijʌ `bʊdʊt nʌ `etʌj n'e`d'el'e]

781. What is on in the theaters? – **Ка`кие `пьесы сей`час и`дут в те`атрах?** [kʌ`k'ie p`jesy sej`tʃʌs id`ʊt v t'e`ʌtrʌh]

782. What is the best drama theater here? – **Ка`кой здесь `лучший драмте`атр?** [kʌ`kɒj zd'es' `lʊtʃʃij drʌmt'e`ʌtr]

783. Where can I attend a ballet? – **Где `можно схо`дить на ба`лет?** [gd'e `mɒʒnʌ shʌ`d'it' nʌ bʌ`l'et]

784. Where can I attend an opera? – **Где `можно пос`лушать `оперу?** [gd'e `mɒʒnʌ pʌs`lʊʃʌt' `ɒp'erʊ]

785. Who are the leading singers? – **Кто ве`дущие со`листы?** [ktɒ v'e`dʊʃ'ije sʌ`l'isty]

786. Who are the leading dancers? – **Кто ве`дущие тан`цоры-со`листы?** [ktɒ v'e`dʊʃ'ije tʌnt`sɒry sʌ`l'isty]

787. Who is the conductor today? – **Кто се`годня дири`жирует?** [ktɒ s'e`vɒdn'ʌ d'ir'i`ʒirʊjet]

788. Are there any festivals going on now? – **Сей`час `идут ка`кие-нибудь фести`вали?** [ʃej`tʃʌs 'i`dʊt kʌ`k'ijen'ibʊd' f'est'i`vʌl'i]

789. Where can I attend a rock concert / pop concert? – **Где `можно схо`дить на рок кон`церт / поп кон`церт?** [gd'e `mɒʒnʌ shʌd'it' nʌ rɒk kʌn`sert / pɒp kʌn`sert]

790. Is there any place where they play jazz? – **Тут `где-нибудь `можно пос`лушать джаз?** [tʊt g`d'en'ibʊd' `mɒʒnʌ pʌs`lʊʃʌt' dʒʌz]

791. Where can I listen to classical music? – **Где `можно пос`лушать клас`сическую `музыку?** [gd'e `mɒʒnʌ pʃs`lʊʃʌt' klʌ`s'itʃeskʊjʊ `mʊzykʊ]

792. I need a place in the stalls – **Мне ˋнужно ˋместо в парˋтере** [mn'e ˋnuʒnʌ ˋm'estʌ v pʌrˋt'er'e]

793. I need a place in the dress circle – **Мне ˋнужно ˋместо в бельэтаˋже** [mn'e ˋnuʒnʌ ˋm'estʌ v b'el'eˋtʌʒe]

794. I need a place in the first / second / third circle – **Мне ˋнужно ˋместо на ˋпервом / втоˋром / тˋретьем ˋярусе** [mn'e ˋnuʒnʌ ˋm'estʌ nʌ ˋp'ervʌm / vtʌˋrɒm / tˋr'etjem ˋjʌrus'e]

795. I need a place on the balcony – **Мне ˋнужно ˋместо на балˋконе** [mn'e ˋnuʒnʌ ˋm'estʌ nʌ bʌlˋkɒn'e]

796. I need a general admission ticket – **Мне ˋнужен входˋной биˋлет** [mn'e ˋnuʒen vhʌdnɒj b'iˋl'et]

797. I need a place in the first row – **Мне ˋнужно ˋместо в ˋпервом ряˋду** [mn'e ˋnuʒnʌ ˋm'estʌ v ˋp'ervʌm r'ʌˋdu]

798. What is the place with the best view? – **На каˋких месˋтах ˋсамый ˋлучший вид?** [nʌ kʌˋk'ih m'esˋtʌh ˋsʌmyj ˋlutʃʃij v'id]

799. I would like to book ... tickets – **Я хоˋчу ˋзаказать ...** [jʌ hʌˋtʃu zʌkʌˋzʌt' ...]

 - After any numeral ending with 1 – except 11 – **биˋлет** [b'iˋl'et]

 - After any numeral ending with 2, 3, 4 – except 12, 13, 14 – **биˋлета** [b'iˋl'ˋetʌ]

 - After the numerals 11-14 or any numeral ending with 0, 5, 6, 7, 8, 9 – **биˋлетов** [b'il'ˋetʌf]

See Numerals

800. Sorry, we are fully booked – **Извиˋните, все биˋлеты пˋроданы** [ˋɪzv"iˋn'it'e fse b'iˋl'ety pˋrɒdʌny]

801. How many acts are in this play? – С`колько `актов в `этой `пьесе? [s`kɒl'kʌ `ʌktʌf v `etʌj `pjes'e]

802. What films are on now? – Ка`кие `фильмы сей`час в про`кате? [kʌ`k'ie `f'il'my sej`tʃʌs v prʌ`kʌt'e]

803. Which cinema do you recommend me to go to? – В ка`кой киноте`атр посо`ветуете пой`ти? [v kʌ`kɒj k'inʌt'e`ʌtr pʌsʌ`v'etʊjet'e pʌj`t'i]

804. What film is it worth seeing? – Ка`кой фильм с`тоит посмот`реть? [kʌ`kɒj f'il'm s`tɒ'it pʌsmʌt`r'et']

805. Is it a Russian film? – `Это `русский фильм? [`etʌ `rʊsk'ij f'il'm]

806. Who is the director? – Кто режис`сёр? [ktɒ reʒ'i`s'ɒr]

807. Who are the leading actors? – Кто в г`лавных ро`лях? [ktɒ v g`lʌvnyh rʌ`l'ʌh]

808. Is it the premiere? – `Это пре`мьера? [`etʌ pr'e`mjerʌ]

809. What language is this movie showing in? – На ка`ком язы`ке демонст`рируется `этот фильм? [nʌ kʌ`kɒm jʌzy`k'e demʌnst`r'irʊjetsʌ `etʌt f'il'm]

810. Is this movie showing with subtitles? – `Этот фильм демонст`рируется с суб`титрами? [`etʌt f'il'm demʌnst`r'irʊjetsʌ s sʊb`t'itrʌm'i]

811. Is this movie showing with the voiceover? – `Этот фильм демонст`рируется с оз`вучкой? [`etʌt f'il'm demʌnst`r'irʊjetsʌ s ʌz`vʊtʃkʌj]

812. I would like to see a / an ... – Я хо`чу посмот`реть ... [jʌ hʌ`tʃʊ pʌsmʌt`r'et'...]

813. ... Detective film – детек`тив [detek`t'if]

814. ... Drama - д`раму [d`rʌmʊ]

815. ... Comedy - ко`медию [kʌ`m'ed'ijʊ]

816. ... Horror movie - `ужасы [`ʊʒʌsy]

817. ... Indie film - `авторское ки`но [`ʌftʌrskʌje ki`nɒ]

818. ... Thriller - т`риллер [t`r'il'er]

819. ... Science-fiction film - на`учную фан`тастику [nʌ`ʊtʃnʊjʊ fʌn`tʌst'ikʊ]

820. Where can I buy popcorn? - Где `можно ку`пить поп`корн? [gd'e `mɒʒnʌ kʊ`p'it' pʌp`kɒrn]

821. I would like a place somewhere in the middle - Мне, по`жалуйста, `место в сере`дине [mn'e pʌ`ʒʌlʊstʌ `m'estʌ v s'er'e`d'in'e]

822. I have already seen this movie - Я у`же `видел (masculine) / `видела (feminine) `этот фильм [jʌ ʊ`ʒe `v'id'el / `v'id'elʌ `etʌt f'il'm]

6.2. Inside a Museum or Theater, Etc.

823. Where is the entrance? - Где вход? [gd'e vhɒt]

824. Where is the main entrance? - Где г`лавный в`ход? [gd'e g`lʌvnyj vhɒt]

825. What are the opening hours of the museum? - По ка`ким дням и в ка`кие ча`сы ра`ботает му`зей? [pʌ kʌ`k'im dn'ʌm i v kʌ`k'ie tʃʌ`sy rʌ`bɒtʌjet mʊ`zej]

826. Excuse me, is it the queue to ...? - Изви`ните, `это `очередь в...? [`ɪzv'i`n'it'e `etʌ `ɒtʃ'er'ed' v...]

827. Give me ... tickets please - `Дайте, по`жалуйста ... [`dʌjt'e pʌ`ʒʌlʊstʌ ...]

 - After any numeral ending with 1 - except 11 - би`лет [b'i`l'et]

- After any numeral ending with 2, 3, 4 - except 12, 13, 14 - би`лета [b'i`l'etʌ]

- After the numerals 11-14 or any numeral ending with 0, 5, 6, 7, 8, 9 - би`летов [b'il'`etʌf]

See Numerals

828. I need a child / adult ticket - Мне `нужен `детский / вз`рослый би`лет [mn'e `nuʒen `d'etsk'ij / vz`rɒslyj b'i`l'et]

829. When does the museum open / close? - Ког`да откры`вается / закры`вается му`зей? [kʌg`dʌ ʌtkry`vʌjetsʌ / zʌkry`vʌjetsʌ mu`zej]

830. Where is the cloakroom? - Где на`ходится гарде`роб? [gd'e nʌ`hɒd'itsʌ gʌrd'e`rɒp]

831. Can I leave this bag in the cloakroom? - `Можно ос`тавить в гарде`робе `эту `сумку / свой `зонтик / рюк`зак? [`mɒʒnʌ ʌs`tʌv'it' v gʌrd'e`rɒb'e `etu `sumku / svɒj `zɒnt'ik / r'uk`zʌk]

832. Can I rent a pair of opera glasses? - `Можно взять напро`кат би`нокль? [`mɒʒnʌ vz'ʌt' nʌprʌ`kʌt b'i`nɒkl']

833. How much does the rental of opera glasses cost? - С`колько с`тоит а`ренда би`нокля? [s`kɒl'kʌ s`tɒ'it ʌ`r'endʌ b'i`nɒkl'ʌ]

834. Can I rent a special child seat? - `Можно взять напро`кат `детское си`дение? [`mɒʒnʌ vz'ʌt' nʌprʌ`kʌt `d'etskʌje s'i`d'en'je]

835. I have lost my cloakroom ticket - Я поте`рял (masculine) / поте`ряла (feminine) свой номе`рок [jʌ pʌt'e`r'ʌl / pʌt'er`ʌlʌ svɒj nʌm'er`ɒk]

836. Where is the toilet situated? - Где на`ходится туа`лет? [gd'e nʌ`hɒd'itsʌ tuʌ`l'et]

837. Is there a museum information brochure? – **В му`зее `можно взять информаци`онный бук`лет?** [v mʊ`z'eje `mɒʒnʌ vz'ʌt' infʌrmʌts'i`ɒnyj bʊk`l'et]

838. Can I take photos inside? – **`Можно ли внут`ри фотогра`фировать?** [`mɒʒnʌ l'i vnʊ`tr'i fʌtʌgrʌ`f'irʌvʌt']

839. Photography is not permitted – **Фотогра`фировать запреще`но** [fʌtʌgrʌ`f'irʌvʌt' zʌpr'eʃ'enʌ]

840. Flash photography is not permitted – **Фото`съёмка со вс`пышкой запреще`на** [fʌtʌ`sjɒmkʌ sʌ vs`pyʃkʌj zʌpreʃ'e`nʌ]

841. Photography costs ... – **Фото`съёмка с`тоит ...** [fʌtʌ`sjɒmkʌ s`tɒ'it ...] – **See Finances**

842. Smoking is not permitted – **Ку`рить запре`щается** [kʊr'it' zʌp`reʃʌjetsʌ]

843. Please do not touch – **По`жалуйста, не `трогайте** [pʌ`ʒʌlʊstʌ n'e t`rɒgʌjt'e]

844. We ask you to turn off all cell phones – **П`росим вас `выключить сво`и мо`бильные теле`фоны** [p`rɒs'im vʌs `vyklʊtʃ'it' svʌ`i mʌ`b'il'nyje t'el'e`fɒny]

845. Please turn all mobile phones off during the performance – **По`жалуйста, на в`ремя представ`ления отклю`чите мо`бильные теле`фоны** [pʌ`ʒʌlʊstʌ nʌ v`r'em'ʌ pr'edstʌv`l'en'ijʌ ʌtk`lʊtʃ'it'e mʌ`b'il'nyje t'el'e`fɒny]

846. Where can I buy the theater programme? – **Где `можно ку`пить прог`раммку?** [gd'e `mɒʒnʌ kʊ`p'it' prʌg`rʌmkʊ]

847. How much is the theater programme? – **С`колько с`тоит прог`раммка?** [s`kɒl'kʌ s`tɒ'it prʌg`rʌmkʌ]

848. Excuse me, have you got a theater programme? – **Изви`ните, у вас нет прог`раммки?** [ɪzv'i`n'it'e ʊ vʌs n'et prʌg`rʌmk'i]

849. Can I borrow your theater programme for a minute? – **`Можно одол`жить у вас прог`раммку на ми`нуту?** [`mɒʒnʌ ʌdʌlʒ'it' ʊ vʌs prʌg`rʌmkʊ nʌ m'i`nʊtʊ?]

850. Will there be an intermission? – **`Будет ли ант`ракт?** [`bʊd'et l'i ʌnt`rʌkt]

851. How long is the intermission? – **С`колько д`лится ант`ракт?** [s`kɒl'kʌ d`l'itsʌ ʌnt`rʌkt]

(Note that in Russian theaters, they use the system of **three bells** to mark the time left before the beginning of a performance; thus, you can hear one, two, or three short bells – usually together with a loud announcement at the very beginning of an evening or during the intermission; the first single bell means that there are fifteen minutes left before the beginning of the show and they have opened the doors to the audience space, the second double bell marks five minutes before the beginning – here you must hurry up and go to your seat, and the third triple bell means that the performance is about to start, the doors to the audience space will be closed and no spectators will be allowed to get in.)

852. The first / second / third bell has sounded – **Был дан `первый / вто`рой / т`ретий зво`нок** [bʌl dʌn p'er`vyj / vtʌ`rɒj / t`r'et'ij zvʌ`nɒk]

853. Is there a café here? – **Здесь есть ка`фе?** [zd'es' jest' kʌ`fe]

854. Where is the café situated? – **Где на`ходится ка`фе?** [gd'e nʌ`hɒd'itsʌ kʌ`fe]

855. Where is the exhibition …? – **Где на`ходится `выставка …?** [gd'e nʌ`hɒd'itsʌ `vystʌfkʌ …]

856. The exhibition ... is on the first / second / third / fourth / fifth floor - **`Выставка ... на`ходится на `первом / вто`ром / т`ретьем / чет`вёртом / `пятом эта`же** [`vystʌfkʌ ... nʌ`hɒd'itsʌ nʌ `p'ervʌm / vtʌ`rɒm / t`ret'jem / tʃet`v'ɒrtʌm / `p'ʌtʌm etʌ`ʒe] See **Numerals**

857. Is there a souvenir shop? - **Здесь есть суве`нирный мага`зин?** [zd'es' jest' sʊv'e`n'irnyj mʌgʌ`z'in]

858. Are there any guided tours? - **У вас про`водятся экс`курсии?** [ʊ vʌs prʌ`vɒd'ʌtsʌ eks`kʊrs'ii]

859. How much is the guided tour? - **С`колько с`тоит экс`курсия?** [s`kɒl'kʌ s`tɒ'it eks`kʊrs'ijʌ]

860. When does the guided tour start / end? - **Ког`да начи`нается / за`канчивается экс`курсия?** [kʌg`dʌ nʌtʃ'i`nʌjetsʌ / zʌ`kʌntʃ'ivʌjetsʌ eks`kʊrs'ijʌ]

861. Where is the assembly point for this guided tour? - **Где на`ходится `место сбора для `этой экс`курсии?** [gd'e nʌ`hɒd'itsʌ `m'estʌ s`bɒrʌ dl'ʌ `etʌj eks`kʊrs'ii]

862. Is there an audio guide? - **У вас есть аудио`гид?** [ʊ vʌs jest' ʌʊd'iɒ`g'id]

863. What languages does your audio guide support? - **На ка`ких язы`ках дос`тупны аудио`гиды?** [nʌ kʌ`k'ih jʌzy`kʌh dʌs`tʊpny ʌʊd'iɒ`g'idy]

864. Can I rent a / an ... audio guide? - **`Можно ли взять аудио`гид на ...** [`mɒʒnʌ l'i vz'ʌt' ʌʊd'iɒ`g'id nʌ ...]

865. ... Chinese - **ки`тайском** [k'i`tʌjskʌm]

866. ... English - **анг`лийском** [ʌng`l'ijskʌm]

867. ... French - **фран`цузском** [frʌn`tsʊskʌm]

868. ... German - **не`мецком** [n'e`m'etskʌm]

869. ... Italian - ита`льянском ['itʌ`l'jʌnskʌm]

870. ... Japanese - я`понском [jʌ`pɒnskʌm]

871. ... Spanish - ис`панском [is`pʌnskʌm]

872. What is this thing? - Что `это та`кое? [ʃtɒ `etʌ tʌ`kɒje]

873. This is a ... - `Это ... [`etʌ]

874. ... Landscape - пей`заж [p´ej`zʌʒ]

875. ... Oil painting - кар`тина `маслом [kʌr`t'inʌ `mʌslʌm]

876. ... Ornament - укра`шение [ʊkrʌ`ʃen'ije]

877. ... Piece of jewelry - драго`ценность [drʌgʌ`tsenʌst']

878. ... Portrait - порт`рет [pʌrt`r'et]

879. ... Pottery - ке`рамика [k´e`rʌm'ikʌ]

880. ... Sculpture - скульп`тура [skʊl'p`tʊrʌ]

881. ... Still life - натюр`морт [nʌt´ʊr`mɒrt]

882. ... Tapestry - гобе`лен [gʌb´e`l'en]

883. ... Watercolour - аква`рель [ʌkvʌ`r'el']

884. Can you tell me about this thing? - Расска`жите, по`жалуйста, об `этой `вещи [rʌskʌ`ʒit'e pʌ`ʒʌlʊstʌ ʌb `etʌj `v'eʃ'i]

885. How old is this thing? - С`колько лет `этой `вещи? [s`kɒl'kʌ let `etʌj `v'eʃ'i]

886. Who painted this picture? - Кто напи`сал эту кар`тину? [ktɒ nʌp'i`sʌl `etʊ kʌr`t'inʊ]

887. Whose portrait is this? - Чей `это порт`рет? [tʃej `etʌ pʌrt`r'et]

888. Can you show me other works of this artist? - **`Можете пока`зать д`ругие ра`боты `этого ху`дожника?** [`mɒʒet'e pʌkʌ`zʌt' drʊ`g'ije rʌ`bɒty `etʌvʌ hʊ`dɒʒn'ikʌ]

889. What style is it? - **Какой `это стиль?** [kʌ`kɒj `etʌ st'il']

890. Is it the original or a replica? - **`Это ориги`нал или `копия?** [`etʌ ʌr'ig'i`nʌl il'i `kɒp'ijʌ]

891. When was this picture painted? - **Ког`да бы`ла на`писана `эта картина?** [kʌg`dʌ by`lʌ nʌ`p'isʌnʌ `etʌ kʌr`t'inʌ]

892. Could you tell me more about the artist? - **Расска`жите, по`жалуйста, попод`робнее об `этом ху`дожнике** [rʌskʌ`ʒ'it'e pʌ`ʒʌlʊstʌ pʌpʌd`rɒbn'eje ʌb `etʌm hʊ`dɒʒn'ik'e]

893. Quiet please - **По`жалуйста, соблю`дайте тиши`ну** [pʌ`ʒʌlʊstʌ sʌbl'ʊ`dʌjt'e t'iʃi`nʊ]

894. Please, keep away from the exhibit / display case - **По`жалуйста, не подхо`дите с`лишком б`лизко к экспо`нату / вит`рине** [pʌ`ʒʌlʊstʌ n'e pʌdhʌ`d'it'e s`l'iʃkʌm b`l'iakʌ k ekspʌ`nʌtʊ / v'it`r'in'e]

895. All visitors are requested to proceed to the exit - **П`росим всех посе`тителей прой`ти к `выходу** [p`rɒs'im vs'eh pʌs'et'it'e`lej prʌj`t'i k `vyhʌdʊ]

896. The museum is closing in half an hour - **Му`зей закры`вается `через полча`са** [mʊ`z'ej zʌkry`vʌjetsʌ `tʃerez `pɒltʃʌsʌ]

897. The museum is closing in ... minutes - **Музей закры`вается `через ...** [mʊ`z'ej zʌkry`vʌjetsʌ `tʃerez ...]

- After any numeral ending with 1 - except 11 - **ми`нуту** [m'i`nʊtʊ]

- After any numeral ending with 2, 3, 4 – except 12, 13, 14 – **ми`нуты** [m'i`nʋty]

- After the numerals 11-14 or any numeral ending with 0, 5, 6, 7, 8, 9 – **ми`нут** [m'i`nʋt]

See Numerals

898. Where is the exit? – **Где `выход?** [gd'e `vyhʌt]

Chapter 7. Shopping and Banking

7.1. Finances

899. I have some money – У ме`ня есть `деньги [υ m'e`n'ʌ jest' `d'en'g'i]

900. I have no money – У ме`ня нет `денег [υ m'e`n'ʌ n'et `d'en'ek]

901. I have run out of money – У ме`ня `кончились `деньги [υ m'e`n'ʌ `kɒntʃ'il'is' `d'en'g'i]

902. I have some coins – У ме`ня есть мо`неты [υ m'e`n'ʌ jest' mʌ`n'ety]

903. I have not got any coins – У ме`ня нет мо`нет [υ m'e`n'ʌ n'et mʌ`n'et]

904. I only have banknotes – У ме`ня `только ку`пюры [υ m'e`n'ʌ `tɒl'kʌ kυ`p'υry]

905. Have you got any change? – У вас `будет с`дача? [υ vʌs `bυd'et s`dʌtʃʌ]

906. I have not got any change, sorry – У ме`ня не `будет с`дачи, изви`ните [υ m'e`n'ʌ n'e `bυd'et s`dʌtʃ'i 'izv'i`n'it'e]

907. Have you got roubles / dollars / euros / pounds? – У вас есть руб`ли / `доллары / `евро / `фунты? [υ vʌs jest' rυb`l'i / `dɒllʌry / `jevrʌ / `fυnty]

(Note that the currency of the Russian Federation is rouble – **рубль** [rʊbl], the rouble is subdivided into 100 kopeks – **ко`пейка** [kʌ`p'ejkʌ]; kopeks are produced in the form of 1-, 5-, 10-, 50-kopek coins, while roubles are produced in the form of 1-, 2-, 5-, 10-rouble coins as well as 5- and 10-rouble banknotes, which are almost out of circulation, as well as common and widely used 50-, 100-, 200-, 500-, 1000-, 2000-, 5000-rouble banknotes.

908. There are ... rouble(s) and ... kopek(s) – **Тут** ... [tʊt ...]

- After any numeral ending with 1 – except 11 – **рубль / ко`пейка** [rʊbl' / kʌ`p'ejkʌ]

- After any numeral ending with 2, 3, 4 – except 12, 13, 14 – **руб`ля / ко`пейки** [rʊb`l'ʌ / kʌ`p'ejk'i]

- After the numerals 11-14 or any numeral ending with 0, 5, 6, 7, 8, 9 – **руб`лей / ко`пеек** [rʊb`l'ej / kʌ`p'ejek]

See Numerals

909. There are ... dollars – **Тут** ... [tʊt ...]

- After any numeral ending with 1 – except 11 – **`доллар** [`dɒlʌr]

- After any numeral ending with 2, 3, 4 – except 12, 13, 14 – **`доллара** [`dɒlʌrʌ]

- After the numerals 11-14 or any numeral ending with 0, 5, 6, 7, 8, 9 – **`долларов** [`dɒlʌrʌf]

See Numerals

910. There are ... euros – **Тут** ... [tʊt ...]

- After any numeral ending with 1 – except 11 – **`евро** [`jevrʌ]

- After any numeral ending with 2, 3, 4 – except 12, 13, 14 – **`евро** [`jevrʌ]

- After the numerals 11-14 or any numeral ending with 0, 5, 6, 7, 8, 9 - `евро [`jevrʌ]

See Numerals

911. There are ... pounds - **Тут ...** [tʊt ...]

- After any numeral ending with 1 - except 11 - `фунт [`fʊnt]

- After any numeral ending with 2, 3, 4 - except 12, 13, 14 - `фунта [`fʊntʌ]

- After the numerals 11-14 or any numeral ending with 0, 5, 6, 7, 8, 9 - `фунтов [`fʊntʌf]

See Numerals

912. Where is a currency exchange situated? - **Где на`ходится об`мен ва`люты?** [gd'e nʌ`hɒd'itsʌ ʌb`m'en vʌ`l'ʊty]

913. I would like to exchange some money - **Я хо`чу обме`нять деньги** [ʌ hʌ`tʃʊ ʌbm'e`n'ʌt' `d'en'g'i]

914. What is the exchange rate? - **Ка`кой курс?** [kʌ`kɒj kʊrs]

915. Could you give me some smaller banknotes? - **Если `можно, `дайте, по`жалуйста, `мелкими банк`нотами** [`jesl'i `mɒʒnʌ `dʌjt'e pʌ`ʒʌlʊstʌ `m'elk'im'i bʌnk`nɒtʌm'i]

916. I would like to pay this in - **Я хо`чу внес`ти `это на счёт** [jʌ hʌ`tʃʊ vn'es`t'i `etʌ nʌ ʃ'ɒt]

917. I would like to know my balance - **Я хо`чу уз`нать свой ба`ланс** [jʌ hʌ`tʃʊ ʊz`nʌt' svɒj bʌ`lʌns]

918. Fill in this form please - **За`полните, по`жалуйста, `эту `форму** [zʌ`pɒln'it'e pʌ`ʒʌlʊstʌ `etʊ `fɒrmʊ]

919. Have you got any ID with you? – **У вас есть с со`бой ка`кое-нибудь удостове`рение `личности?** [ʊ vʌs jest' s sʌ`bɒj kʌ`kɒjen'ibʊd' ʊdʌstʌv'e`r'en'ije `l'itʃnʌst'i]

920. I have not got any cash – **У ме`ня нет на`личных** [ʊ m'e`n'ʌ n'et nʌ`l'itʃnyh]

921. Can I pay by cash? – **`Можно опла`тить на`личными?** [`mɒʒnʌ ʌplʌ`t'it' nʌ`l'itʃnym'i]

922. Can I pay by card? – **`Можно ли опла`тить `картой?** [`mɒʒnʌ ʌplʌ`t'it' `kʌrtʌj]

923. I have a credit / debit card – **У ме`ня кре`дитная / `дебетовая `карта** [ʊ m'e`n'ʌ kr'e`d'itnʌjʌ / `deb'etʌvʌjʌ `kʌrtʌ]

924. Sorry, we do not accept cards – **Изви`ните, мы не прини`маем `карты** ['ɪzv'i`n'it'e my n'e pr'in'i`mʌjem `kʌrty]

925. This card is not accepted – **`Эта `карта не прини`мается** [`etʌ `kʌrtʌ n'e pr'in'i`mʌjetsʌ]

926. The operation has been declined by the bank – **Опе`рация отклоне`на `банком** [ʌp'e`rʌts'ijʌ ʌtklʌn'e`nʌ `bʌnkʌm]

927. Insufficient funds – **Недос`таточно с`редств** [n'edʌs`tʌtʌtʃnʌ s`r'etstf]

928. The commission is ... percent – **Ко`миссия сос`тавит ...** [kʌ`m'is'ijʌ sʌs`tʌv'it ...]

- After any numeral ending with 1 – except 11 – **про`цент** [prʌ`tsent]

- After any numeral ending with 2, 3, 4 – except 12, 13, 14 – **про`цента** [prʌ`tsentʌ]

- After the numerals 11-14 or any numeral ending with 0, 5, 6, 7, 8, 9 – **про`центов** [prʌ`tsentʌf]

See Numerals

929. No commission - Без ко`миссии [bez kʌ`m'is'ii]

930. I have lost my wallet - Я поте`рял (masculine) / поте`ряла (feminine) коше`лёк [jʌ pʌt'e`r'ʌl / pʌt'e`r'ʌlʌ kʌʃe`lɒk]

931. Where is a bank situated? - Где на`ходится банк? [gd'e nʌ`hɒd'itsʌ bʌnk]

932. Where is the nearest ATM? - Где на`ходится бли`жайший банко`мат? [gd'e nʌ`hɒd'itsʌ bl'i`ʒʌjʃij bʌnkʌ`mʌt]

933. Choose a language - `Выберите я`зык [`vyb'er'it'e jʌ`zyk]

934. Cancel - От`мена [ʌt`m'enʌ]

935. Please wait - По`жалуйста, подож`дите [pʌ`ʒʌlʊstʌ pʌdʌʒ`d'it'e]

936. Withdraw money - Снять `деньги [sn'ʌt' `d'en'g'i]

937. Deposit money - Внес`ти `деньги [vn'es`t'i `d'en'g'i]

938. Transfer money - Перевес`ти `деньги [p'er'ev'es`t'i `d'en'g'i]

939. I need help with this ATM - Помо`гите мне, по`жалуйста, с банко`матом [pʌmʌ`g'it'e mn'e pʌ`ʒʌlʊstʌ s bʌnkʌ`mʌtʌm]

940. How much do you earn? - С`колько вы зара`батываете? [s`kɒl'kʌ vy zʌrʌ`bʌtyvʌjet'e]

941. I earn ... per month / per year - Я зара`батываю ... в `месяц / в год [jʌ zʌrʌ`bʌtyvʌjʊ ... v `m'esʌts / v gɒt]
See Numerals

942. I do not want to spend much much money - **Я не хо`чу т`ратить м`ного `денег** [jʌ n'e hʌ`ʧʊ t`rʌt'it' m`nɒgʌ `d'en'ek]

943. I have spent too much money - **Я пот`ратил** (masculine) / **пот`ратила** (feminine) **м`ного `денег** [jʌ pʌt`rʌt'il / pʌt`rʌt'ilʌ m`nɒgʌ `d'en'ek]

944. I want to invest some money - **Я хо`чу инвес`тировать** [jʌ hʌ`ʧʊ inv'es`t'irʌvʌt']

945. I need a consultant - **Мне `нужен консуль`тант** [mn'e `nʊʒen kʌnsʊl'`tʌnt]

7.1. General shopping

946. Where can I go shopping here? - **Где здесь `можно уст`роить `шоппинг?** [gd'e zdes' `mɒʒnʌ ʊst`rɒ'it' `ʃɒp'ing]

947. I would like to go shopping - **Мне хо`телось бы похо`дить по мага`зинам** [mn'e hʌ`t'elʌs' by pʌhʌ`d'it' pʌ mʌgʌ`z'inʌm]

948. I (do not) like shopping - **Мне (не) н`равится хо`дить по мага`зинам** [mn'e (n'e) n`rʌv'itsʌ hʌd'it' pʌ mʌgʌ`z'inʌm]

949. Where can I buy ...? - **Где `можно ку`пить ...?** [gd'e `mɒʒnʌ kʊ`p'it' ...]

950. ... Alcoholic beverages - **Алко`голь** [ʌlkʌ`gɒl']

951. ... Bakery goods - **`Выпечку** [`vyp'etʃkʊ]

952. ... Books - **К`ниги** [k`n'ig'i]

953. ... Children's products - **То`вары для де`тей** [tʌ`vʌry dl'ʌ d'e`t'ej]

954. ... Clothes - **О`дежду** [ʌ`d'eʒdʊ]

955. ... Confectionery - **Кон`дитерские из`делия** [kʌn`d'it'ersk'ije 'iz`d'el'ijʌ]

956. ... Cosmetics - **Кос`метику** [kʌs`m'et'ikʋ]

957. ... Crockery - **По`суду** [pʌ`sʋdʋ]

958. ... Flowers - **Цве`ты** [tʃv'e`ty]

959. ... Food - **Е`ду** [je`dʋ]
See Food

960. ... Household appliances - **Быто`вую `технику** [bytʌ`vʋjʋ `t'ehn'ikʋ]

961. ... House-cleaning and laundry products - **Быто`вую `химию** [bytʌ`vʋjʋ `h'im'ijʋ]

962. ... Jewelry - **Юве`лирные из`делия** [jʋv'e`l'irnyje 'iz`d'el'ijʌ]

963. ... Personal hygiene and grooming products - **Пред`меты `личной гиги`ены** [pr'ed`m'ety `l'itʃnʌj g'ig'i`jeny]

964. ... Pet products - **То`вары для жи`вотных** [tʌ`vʌry dl'ʌ ʒ'i`vɒtnyh]

965. ... Pharmaceuticals - **Ле`карства** [l'e`kʌrstvʌ]

966. ... Porcelain - **Фар`фор** [fʌr`fɒr]

967. ... Souvenirs - **Суве`ниры** [sʋv'e`n'iry]

968. ... Toys - **Иг`рушки** [ɪg`rʋʃk'i]

969. Where is the nearest ...? - **Где поб`лизости на`ходится ...?** [gd'e pʌb`l'izʌst'i nʌ`hɒd'itsʌ ...]

970. ... Bookshop - **К`нижный мага`зин** [k`n'iʒnyj mʌgʌ`z'in]

971. ... Butcher's - **Мяс`ной мага`зин** [m'ʌs`nɒj mʌgʌ`z'in]

972. ... Clothes store - **Мага`зин о`дежды** [mʌgʌ`z'in ʌ`d'eʒdy]

973. ... Dairy - **Мо`лочный мага`зин** [mʌ`lɒtʃnyj mʌgʌ`z'in]

974. ... Department store - **Универ`маг** [ʊn'iv'er`mʌg]

975. ... Florist's - **Цве`точный мага`зин** [tʃv'e`tɒtʃnyj mʌgʌ`z'in]

976. ... Fishmonger's - **`Рыбный мага`зин** [`rybnyj mʌgʌ`z'in]

977. ... Greengrocer's - **Мага`зин `овощи-ф`рукты** [mʌgʌ`z'in `ɒvʌʃ'i f`rʊkty]

978. ... Grocery - **Продук`товый мага`зин** [prʌdʊk`tɒvyj mʌgʌ`z'in]

979. ... Hypermarket - **Гипер`маркет** [g'ip'er`mʌrk'et]

980. ... Jeweler's - **Юве`лирный мага`зин** [jʊv'e`l'irnyj mʌgʌ`z'in]

981. ... Mall - **Тор`говый центр** [tʌr`gɒvyj tsentr]

982. ... Market - **`Рынок** [`rynʌk]

983. ... Optician's - **`Оптика** [`ɒpt'ikʌ]

984. ... Outlet - **Аут`лет** [ʌʊt`l'et]

985. ... Pet shop - **То`вары для жи`вотных** [tʌ`vʌry dl'ʌ ʒ'i`vɒtnyh]

986. ... Pharmacy - **Ап`тека** [ʌp`t'ekʌ]

987. ... Shoe shop - **Мага`зин `обуви** [mʌgʌ`z'in `ɒbʊv'i]

988. ... Stationery shop - **Канце`лярский мага`зин** [kʌntse`l'ʌrsk'ij mʌgʌ`z'in]

989. ...Supermarket - **Супер`маркет** [sʊp'er`mʌrket]

990. ...Toy shop - **Мага`зин иг`рушек** [mʌgʌ`z'in 'ig`rʊʃek]

991. I need a shopping trolley - **Мне нуж`на те`лежка** [mn'e nʊʒ`nʌ t'e`l'eʒkʌ]

992. I need a shopping basket - **Мне нуж`на кор`зинка** [mn'e nʊʒ`nʌ kʌr`z'inkʌ]

993. Sale - **Распро`дажа** [rʌsprʌ`dʌʒʌ]

994. Buy two for the price of one - **Два по це`не одно`го** [dvʌ pʌ tse`n'e ʌdnʌ`vɒ]

995. There are no exchanges or refunds - **Не подле`жит об`мену и возв`рату** [n'e pʌdl'e`ʒ'it ʌb`m'enʊ i vʌzv`rʌtʊ]

996. How much does it cost? - **С`колько `это с`тоит?** [s`kɒl'kʌ `etʌ s`tɒ'it]

997. It is (very) cheap - **`Это (`очень) `дёшево** [`etʌ (`ɒtʃ'en') 'd'ɒʃevʌ]

998. It is (very) expensive - **`Это (`очень) `дорого** [`etʌ (`ɒtʃ'en') `dɒrʌgʌ]

999. It is a high-quality product - **`Это высоко`качественный про`дукт** [`etʌ vysʌkʌ`kʌtʃ'estv'enyj prʌ`dʊkt]

1000. It is handmade - **`Это руч`ная ра`бота** [`etʌ rʊtʃ`nʌjʌ rʌ`bɒtʌ]

1001. There is a discount - **С`кидка** [s`k'itkʌ]

1002. Can I help you? - **Я мо`гу вам `чем-нибудь по`мочь?** [jʌ mʌ`gʊ vʌm `tʃ'emn'ibʊd' pʌ`mɒtʃ]

1003. Thank you, but I am just browsing - **Спа`сибо, я п`росто смот`рю** [spʌ`s'ibʌ jʌ p`rɒstʌ smʌt`r'ʊ]

1004. Excuse me, can you help me? - **Извините, не мог`ли бы вы мне по`мочь?** [ɪzv'i`n'it'e n'e mʌg`l'i by vy mn'e pʌ`mɒtʃ]

1005. Show me this, please – Пока`жите мне `это, по`жалуйста [pʌkʌ`ʒ'it'e mn'e `etʌ pʌ`ʒʌlustʌ]

1006. I will take this to the check-out for you – Я от`несу `это на `кассу [jʌ ʌtn'e`su `etʌ nʌ `kʌsu]

1007. Do you want to take it? – Вы `будете `это брать? [vy `bud'et'e `etʌ brʌt']

1008. Can I try this on? – `Можно `это по`мерить? [`mɒʒnʌ `etʌ pʌ`m'er'it']

1009. Weigh it up please – Вз`весьте, по`жалуйста [vz`v'es't'e pʌ`ʒʌlustʌ]

1010. I need ... grams / kilos – Мне `нужно ... [mn'e `nuʒnʌ ...]

- After any numeral ending with 1 – except 11 – **грамм / килог`рамм** [grʌm / k'ilʌg`rʌm]

- After any numeral ending with 2, 3, 4 – except 12, 13, 14 – **грамма / килог`рамма** [g`rʌmʌ / k'ilʌg`rʌmʌ]

- After the numerals 11-14 or any numeral ending with 0, 5, 6, 7, 8, 9 – **грамм / килог`рамм** [grʌm / k'ilʌg`rʌm]

See **Numerals** and **Measurements**

1011. I need ... items / pairs – Мне `нужно ... [mn'e `nuʒnʌ ...]

- After any numeral ending with 1 – except 11 – **ш`тука / `пара** [ʃ`tukʌ / 'pʌrʌ]

- After any numeral ending with 2, 3, 4 – except 12, 13, 14 – **ш`туки / `пары** [ʃ`tuk'i / 'pʌry]

- After the numerals 11-14 or any numeral ending with 0, 5, 6, 7, 8, 9 – **штук / пар** [ʃtuk / pʌr]

See **Numerals**

1012. Wrap it please – **Завер`ните, по`жалуйста** [zʌv'er`n'it'e pʌ`ʒʌlʊstʌ]

1013. I will take it – **Я `это возь`му** [jʌ `etʌ vʌz''mʊ]

1014. Where is the cash-desk? – **Где на`ходится `касса?** [gd'e nʌ`hɒd'itsʌ `kʌsʌ]

1015. Does it come with a guarantee? – **На `этот то`вар пола`гается га`рантия?** [nʌ `etʌt tʌ`vʌr pʌlʌ`gʌjetsʌ gʌ`rʌnt'ijʌ]

1016. It comes with a / an ... year guarantee – **На `этот то`вар пола`гается ... га`рантии** [nʌ `etʌt tʌ`vʌr pʌlʌ`gʌjetsʌ ... gʌ`rʌnt'ii]

- After any numeral ending with 1 – except 11 – **год** [gɒd]

- After any numeral ending with 2, 3, 4 – except 12, 13, 14 – **`года** [`gɒdʌ]

- After the numerals 11-14 or any numeral ending with 0, 5, 6, 7, 8, 9 – **лет** [l'et]

See Numerals

1017. Can I see it working? – **`Можно посмот`реть, как `это ра`ботает?** [`mɒʒnʌ pʌsmʌt`r'et' kʌk `etʌ rʌ`bɒtʌjet]

1018. Can you write down the price? – **Не мог`ли бы вы напи`сать `цену?** [n'e mʌg`l'i by vy nʌp'i`sʌt' `tsenʊ]

1019. Here is your change – **Вот `ваша с`дача** [vɒt `vʌʃʌ s`dʌtʃʌ]

1020. Give me a receipt, please – **`Дайте чек, по`жалуйста** [`dʌjt'e tʃek pʌ`ʒʌlʊstʌ]

1021. Do you need a bag? – **Вам `нужен па`кет?** [vʌm `nʊʒen pʌ`k'et]

1022. Small or large? – `Маленький или боль`шой? [`mʌl'en'k'ij il'i bʌl'`ʃɒj]

1023. Anything else? – `Что-нибудь е`щё? [ʃ`tɒn'ibʊt' e`ʃ'ɒ]

1024. I will come back later – Я зай`ду по`позже [jʌ zʌj`dʊ pʌ`pɒʒe]

1025. I need to return this – Мне `нужно вер`нуть эту вещь [mn'e `nʊʒnʌ v'er`nʊt' `etʊ v'eʃ']

1026. I would like to return a purchase and get a refund – Я хо`чу вер`нуть эту вещь и полу`чить на`зад сво`и `деньги [jʌ hʌ`tʃʊ v'er`nʊt' `etʊ v'eʃ' i pʌlʊ`tʃ'it' nʌ`zʌd svʌ`i `d'en'g'i]

1027. I bought this here yesterday – Я ку`пил (masculine) / ку`пила (feminine) `эту вещь здесь вче`ра [jʌ kʊ`p'il / kʊ`p'ilʌ `etʊ v'eʃ' zd'es' vtʃ'e`rʌ]

1028. It is broken – `Эта вещь с`ломана [`etʌ v'eʃ' s`lɒmʌnʌ]

1029. It does not work – `Эта вещь не ра`ботает [`etʌ v'eʃ' n'e rʌ`bɒtʌjet]

1030. Can I change it for another thing? – `Можно обме`нять `это на дру`гую вещь? [`mɒʒnʌ l'i ʌbm'e`n'ʌt' `etʌ nʌ drʊ`gʊjʊ veʃ']

1031. Can I get this purchase tax-free? – Пола`гается ли за `эту по`купку такс-фри? [pʌlʌ`gʌjetsʌ l'i zʌ `etʊ pʌ`kʊpkʊ `tʌksfr'i]

7.3. Buying Clothes, Shoes, Accessories, and Jewelry

1032. Where is a fitting room? – Где на`ходится при`мерочная? [gd'e nʌ`hɒd'itsʌ pr'i`m'erʌtʃnʌjʌ]

1033. Have you got a mirror? – У вас есть `зеркало? [ʊ vʌs jest' `z'erkʌlʌ]

1034. I would like another color – **Мне `нужен дру`гой цвет** [mn'e `nuʒen drʊ`gɒj tsv'et]

1035. I need ... color – **Мне `нужен ... цвет** [mn'e `nuʒen ... tsv'et]

1036. ... Beige – **`Бежевый** [`b'eʒevyj]

1037. ... Black – **`Чёрный** [`tʃ'ɒrnyj]

1038. ... Blue (light-blue) – **Голу`бой** [gʌlʊ`bɒj]

1039. ... Brown – **Ко`ричневый** [kʌ`r'itʃn'evyj]

1040. ... Gray – **`Серый** [`s'eryj]

1041. ... Green – **Зе`лёный** [z'e`l'ɒnyj]

1042. ... Orange – **О`ранжевый** [ʌ`rʌnʒevyj]

1043. ... Navy-blue – **`Синий** [`s'in'ij]

1044. ... Pink – **`Розовый** [`rɒzʌvyj]

1045. ... Purple – **Ли`ловый** [l'i`lɒvyj]

1046. ... Red – **К`расный** [k`rʌsnyj]

1047. ... Violet – **Фио`летовый** [f'iʌ`l'etʌvyj]

1048. ... White – **`Белый** [`b'elyj]

1049. ... Yellow – **`Жёлтый** [`ʒ'ɒltyj]

1050. What gem is this? – **Ка`кой `это драго`ценный `камень?** [kʌ`kɒj `etʌ drʌgʌ`tsenyj kʌ`m'en']

1051. This is ... – **`Это ...** [`etʌ ...]

1052. ... Agate – **А`гат** [ʌ`gʌt]

1053. ... Amber – **Ян`тарь** [jʌn`tʌr']

1054. ... Amethyst – **Аме`тист** [ʌm'e`t'ist]

1055. ... Aquamarine – **Аквама`рин** [ʌkvʌmʌ`r'in]

1056. ... Coral – **Ко`ралл** [kʌ`rʌl]

1057. ... Diamond - **Брилли`ант** [br'il'`jʌnt]

1058. ... Emerald - **Изум`руд** [ızʊm`rʊt]

1059. ... Garnet - **Гра`нат** [grʌ`nʌt]

1060. ... Jade - **Неф`рит** [n´efr'it]

1061. ... Lapis lazuli - **`Ляпис-ла`зурь** [`l´ʌp'is lʌ`zʊr']

1062. ... Malachite - **Мала`хит** [mʌlʌ`h'it]

1063. ... Onyx - **`Оникс** [`ɒn'iks]

1064. ... Opal - **О`пал** [ʌ`pʌl]

1065. ... Ruby - **Ру`бин** [rʊ`b'in]

1066. ... Sapphire - **Сап`фир** [sʌp`f'ir]

1067. ... Turquoise - **Бирю`за** [b'ir'ʊ`zʌ]

1068. What metal is this? - **Какой `это ме`талл?** [kʌ`kɒj `etʌ m`e`tʌl]

1069. This is ... - **`Это ...** [`etʌ ...]

1070. ... Aluminium - **Алю`миний** [ʌl´ʊ`m'in'ij]

1071. ... Bronze - **Б`ронза** [b`rɒnzʌ]

1072. ... Copper - **Медь** [m´et']

1073. ... Gold - **`Золото** [`zɒlʌtʌ]

1074. ... Platinum - **П`латина** [p`lʌt'inʌ]

1075. ... Silver - **Сереб`ро** [s´er'eb`rɒ]

1076. ... Steel - **Сталь** [stʌl´]

1077. ... Tin - **`Олово** [`ɒlʌvʌ]

1078. What is it made of? - **Из че`го `это с`делано?** [ız tʃ´e`vɒ `etʌ s`d´elʌnʌ]

1079. The material it is made of is ... - **Матери`ал - ...** [mʌt'er'i`ʌl ...]

1080. ... Cotton - **Х`лопок** [h`lɒpʌk]

1081. ... Fabric - **Т`кань** [tkʌn']

1082. ... Faux leather - **Кожзаме`нитель** [kɒʒzʌm´e`n'it'el']

1083. ... Glass - **Стек`ло** [st'ek`lɒ]

1084. ... Leather - **`Кожа** [`kɒʒʌ]

1085. ... Linen - **Лён** [l'ɒn]

1086. ... Metal - **Ме`талл** [m'e`tʌl]

1087. ... Plastic - **П`ластик** [p`lʌst'ik]

1088. ... Silk - **Шёлк** [ʃɒlk]

1089. ... Stone - **`Камень** [`kʌm'en']

1090. ... Synthetic material - **Син`тетика** [s'in`t'et'ikʌ]

1091. ... Wool - **Шерсть** [ʃerst´]

1092. What is your size? - **Какой у вас размер?** [kʌ`kɒj u vʌs rʌz`m'er]

1093. I need small / medium / large size - **Мне `нужен раз`мер small / medium / large** [mn'e `nuʒen rʌz`m'er ...]

1094. Bring me the small / medium / large size, please - **Прине`сите, по`жалуйста, раз`мер small / medium / large** [pr'in'e`s'it'e pʌ`ʒʌlustʌ rʌz`m'er ...]

1095. This is not my size - **`Это не мой раз`мер** [`etʌ n'e mɒj rʌz`m'er]

1096. It is too loose - **С`лишком сво`бодно** [s`l'iʃkʌm svʌ`bɒdnʌ]

1097. It is too tight - **С`лишком `тесно** [s`l'iʃkʌm t'esnʌ]

1098. It fits well - **Хоро`шо си`дит** [hʌrʌ`ʃɒ s'i`d'it]

1099. This is too big – C`лишком боль`шое [s`lˈiʃkʌm bʌlˈʃɒje]

1100. It is too small – C`лишком `маленькое [s`lˈiʃkʌm `mʌlˈenˈkʌje]

1101. Do you have one size larger / smaller? – У вас есть на раз`мер `больше / `меньше? [u vʌs jestˈ pʌ rʌz`mˈer `bɒlˈʃe / `mˈenˈʃe]

1102. Do you have a … one? – А у вас есть …? [ʌ u vʌs jestˈ …]

1103. … Striped – В по`лоску [u pʌ`lɒsku]

1104. … Polka-dotted – В `горошек [u gʌ`rɒʃek]

1105. … Flowery – В цве`точек [u tsvˈe`tʌtʃˈek]

1106. … Plain – Без у`зора [bˈez u`zɒrʌ]

1107. … Checked – В к`леточку [u k`lˈetʌtʃku]

1108. I am looking for something – have you got a …? – Я `кое-что ищу – у вас есть …? [jʌ `kɒeʃtʌ i`ʃˈu u vʌs jestˈ …]

1109. … Bra – Бюст`гальтер [bˈust`gʌltˈer]

1110. … Cap – `Кепка [`kˈepkʌ]

1111. … Coat – Паль`то [pʌlˈtɒ]

1112. … Dress – П`латье [p`lʌtˈje]

1113. … Dressing gown – Ха`лат [hʌ`lʌt]

1114. … Fleece jacket – Ф`лисовая `куртка [f`lˈisʌvʌjʌ `kurtkʌ]

1115. … Gloves – Пер`чатки [pˈer`tʃʌtkˈi]

1116. … Gym clothes – Спор`тивная о`дежда [spʌr`tˈivnʌjʌ ʌ`dˈeʒdʌ]

1117. … Hat – Ш`ляпа [ʃ`lˈʌpʌ]

1118. ... Hoodie - Толс`товка [tʌls`tɒfkʌ]

1119. ... Jacket - `Куртка [`kʊrtkʌ]

1120. ... Jeans - Д`жинсы [d`ʒynsy]

1121. ... Jumper - Д`жемпер [d`ʒemp'er]

1122. ... Mittens - `Варежки [`vʌr'eʒk'i]

1123. ... Overalls - Комбине`зон [kʌmb'in'e`zɒn]

1124. ... Panties/Underpants - Тру`сы [trʊ`sy]

1125. ... Pajamas - Пи`жама [p'i`ʒʌmʌ]

1126. ... Pullover - Пу`ловер [pʊ`lɒv'er]

1127. ... Raincoat - Плащ [plʌʃ']

1128. ... Scarf - Шарф [ʃʌrf]

1129. ... Shirt - Ру`башка [rʊ`bʌʃkʌ]

1130. ... Shorts - `Шорты [`ʃɒrty]

1131. ... Skirt - `Юбка [`jʊpkʌ]

1132. ... Socks - Нос`ки [nʌs`k'i]

1133. ... Suit - Кос`тюм [kʌs`t'ʊm]

1134. ... Sweater - С`витер [s`v'it'er]

1135. ... Swimming trunks - П`лавки [p`lʌfk'i]

1136. ... Swimsuit (women's) - Ку`пальник [kʊ`pʌl'n'ik]

1137. ... Tights - Когл`готки [kʌgl`gɒtk'i]

1138. ... Top - Топ [tɒp]

1139. ... T-shirt - Фут`болка [fʊt`bɒlkʌ]

1140. ... Trousers - Б`рюки [b`r'ʊk'i]

1141. ... Waistcoat - Жи`лет [ʒ'i`l'et]

1142. ... Warm cap - `Шапка [`ʃʌpkʌ]

1143. Have you got a ... - **У вас есть ...?** [ʊ vʌs jest' ...]

1144. ... Apron - **`Фартук** [`fʌrtʊk]

1145. ... Belt - **Ре`мень** [rʹeˋmʹenʹ]

1146. ... Bow tie - **`Галстук-`бабочка** [`gʌlstʊk `bʌbʌtʃkʌ]

1147. ... Bracelet - **Брас`лет** [brʌsˋlʹet]

1148. ... Brooch - **Брошь** [brɒʃ']

1149. ... Cuff links - **`Запонки** [`zʌpʌnk'i]

1150. ... Earrings - **`Серьги** [`sʹerʹg'i]

1151. ... Glasses - **Оч`ки** [ʌtʃˋk'i]

1152. ... Hair band - **Ре`зинка для во`лос** [rʹeˋz'inkʌ dlʹʌ vʌˋlɒs]

1153. ... Hair grip - **За`колка** [zʌˋkɒlkʌ]

1154. ... Hairpin - **`Шпилька** [ʃˋp'ilʹkʌ]

1155. ... Handbag - **`Сумка** [`sʊmkʌ]

1156. ... Keychain - **Бре`лок** [brʹeˋlɒk]

1157. ... Necklace - **Оже`релье** [ʌʒeˋrʹelʹje]

1158. ... Pendant - **Ку`лон** [kʊˋlɒn]

1159. ... Purse - **Коше`лёк** [kʌʃeˋlʹɒk]

1160. ... Ring - **Коль`цо** [kʌlʹtˋsɒ]

1161. ... Shawl - **Шаль** [ʃʌlʹ]

1162. ... Sunglasses - **`Солнечные оч`ки** [`sɒlnʹetʃnyje ʌtʃˋk'i]

1163. ... Tie - **`Галстук** [`gʌlstʊk]

1164. ... Umbrella - **Зонт** [zɒnt]

1165. ... Wallet - **Бу`мажник** [bʊˋmʌʒn'ik]

1166. ... Watch (Note that this word also means *clock* in Russian) – Ча`сы [tʃʌ`sy]

1167. I want to buy a pair of shoes – Мне `нужно ку`пить `пару бо`тинок [mn'e `nuʒnʌ kup'it' `pʌru bʌ`t'inʌk]

1168. I am looking for – Я и`щу ... [jʌ i`ʃu ...]

1169. ... Boots – Сапо`ги [sʌpʌ`g'i]

1170. ... Flip-flops – Ш`лёпанцы [ʃ`l'ɒpʌntsy]

1171. ... High-heeled shoes – `Туфли на каблу`ке [`tufl'i nʌ kʌblu`k'e]

1172. ... Loafers – Мока`сины [mʌkʌ`s'iny]

1173. ... Sandals (for women) – Босо`ножки [bʌsʌ`nɒʒk'i]

1174. ... Sandals (for men) – Сан`далии [sʌn`dʌl'ii]

1175. ... Shoes – `Туфли [`tufl'i]

1176. ... Sport shoes – Крос`совки [krʌ`sɒfk'i]

1177. These shoes are tight / too large – `Эти бо`тинки мне ма`лы / вели`ки [`et'i bʌ`t'ink'i mn'e mʌ`ly / v'el'i`k'i]

1178. Have you got them in size ...? – У вас есть `эти бо`тинки раз`мера ... [u vʌs jest' `et'i `bʌt'ink'i rʌz`m'erʌ ...]

See Numerals

7.4. Buying Books, Press, Stationery, Souvenirs, and Flowers

1179. Have you got any ... books / newspapers / magazines in – У вас есть ... к`ниги / га`зеты / жур`налы? [u vʌs jest' ... k`n'ig'i / gʌ`z'ety / ʒur`nʌly]

1180. ... Chinese – ки`тайские [k'i`tʌjsk'ije]

1181. ... English - анг`лийские [ʌngˈlˈijskˈije]

1182. ... French - фран`цузские [frʌnˈtsʊskˈije]

1183. ... German - не`мецкие [nˈeˈmˈetskˈije]

1184. ... Italian - ита`льянские [ˈitʌˈlˈjʌnskˈije]

1185. ... Japanese - я`понские [jʌˈpɒnskˈije]

1186. ... Spanish - ис`панские [ˈisˈpʌnskˈije]

1187. Is this a bestseller? - `Это бест`селлер? [ˈetʌ bˈesˈtselˈer]

1188. Is it fiction or non-fiction? - `Это ху`дожественная литера`тура `или на`учно-попу`лярная? [ˈetʌ hʊˈdɒʒestvˈenʌjʌ lˈitˈerʌˈtʊrʌ ilˈi nʌˈʊtʃnʌ pʌpʊˈlˈʌrnʌjʌ]

1189. I need a guidebook on the city of ... - Мне `нужен путево`дитель по `городу ... [mnˈe ˈnʊʒen pʊtˈevʌˈdˈitˈelˈ pʌ ˈgɒrʌdʊ ...]

1190. I need a map of the city of ... - Мне нуж`на карта `города ... [mnˈe nʊʒˈnʌ ˈkʌrtʌ ˈgɒrʌdʌ ...]

1191. I would like to buy a (souvenir) calendar - Я хо`чу ку`пить (суве`нирный) кален`дарь [jʌ hʌˈtʃʊ kʊˈpˈitˈ (sʊvˈeˈnˈirnyj) kʌlˈenˈdʌrˈ]

1192. Where can I find photobooks? - Где `можно най`ти фотоаль`бомы? [gdˈe ˈmɒʒnʌ nʌˈjtˈi ˈfɒtʌ ʌlˈˈbɒmy]

1193. Have you got any comic books? - У вас есть `комиксы? [ʊ vʌs jestˈ ˈkɒmˈiksy]

1194. Where is the children's book department? - Где на`ходится от`дел `детской литера`туры? [gdˈe nʌˈhɒdˈitsʌ ʌˈdˈel ˈdˈetskʌj lˈitˈerʌˈtʊry]

1195. Where can I buy souvenirs? - Где `можно ку`пить суве`ниры? [gdˈe ˈmɒʒnʌ kʊˈpˈitˈ sʊvˈeˈnˈiry]

1196. Are there any books on the history of this city / country? - **У вас есть к`ниги по ис`тории `этого `города / `этой стра`ны?** [u vʌs jest' k`n'ig'i pʌ is`tɒr'ii `etʌvʌ `gɒrʌdʌ / `etʌj strʌ`ny]

1197. Where is the stationery department? - **Где на`ходится от`дел канце`лярских то`варов?** [gd'e nʌ`hɒd'itsʌ ʌt`d'el kʌntse`l'ʌrsk'ih tʌ`vʌrʌf]

1198. I need to buy [a] ... - **Мне `нужно ку`пить ...** [mn'e `nuʒnʌ ku`p'it' ...]

1199. ... Brushes - **`Кисточки** [k'istʌ`tʃk'i]

1200. ... Felt-tip pens - **Фло`мастеры** [flʌ`mʌst'ery]

1201. ... Highlighter - **`Маркер** [`mʌrk'er]

1202. ... Notebook - **Тет`радь** [t'et`rʌt']

1203. ... Notepad - **Блок`нот** [blʌk`nɒt]

1204. ... Paper - **Бу`магу** [bu`mʌgu]

1205. ... Paper clips - **Ск`репки** [sk`r'epk'i]

1206. ... Pen - **`Ручку** [`rutʃku]

1207. ... Pencil - **Каран`даш** [kʌrʌn`dʌʃ]

1208. ... Sketchbook - **Аль`бом** [ʌl'`bɒm]

1209. ... Sticky tape - **Скотч** [skɒtʃ]

1210. ... Stapler - **С`теплер** [s`tepl'er]

1211. I would like to buy some flowers - **Я хо`чу ку`пить цве`ты** [jʌ hʌ`tʃu ku`p'it' tsv'e`ty]

1212. I need a bouquet - **Мне `нужен бу`кет** [mn'e `nuʒen bu`k'et]

1213. Can you make me a bouquet? - **`Можете сос`тавить мне бу`кет?** [`mɒʒet'e sʌs`tʌv'it' mn'e bu`k'et]

1214. Can I choose the flowers? - `Можно я сам (masculine) / са`ма (feminine) `выберу цве`ты? [`mɒznʌ jʌ sʌm / sʌ`mʌ `vyb'erʊ tsv'e`ty]

1215. I would like ... - Мне нуж`ны ... [mn'e nʊʒ`ny ...]

1216. ... Carnations - Гвоз`дики [gvʌz`d'ik'i]

1217. ... Chrysanthemums - Хризан`темы [hr'izʌn`t'emy]

1218. ... Daffodils - Нар`циссы [nʌrt`s'isy]

1219. ... Dahlias - Геор`гины [geʌr`g'iny]

1220. ... Daisies - Марга`ритки [mʌrgʌ`r'itk'i]

1221. ... Gerberas - Гер`беры [g'er`b'ery]

1222. ... Hyacinths - Гиа`цинты [g'iʌ`ts'inty]

1223. ... Irises - `Ирисы [`ɪr'isy]

1224. ... Lilies - `Лилии [`l'il'ii]

1225. ... Orchids - Орхи`деи [ʌrh'i`dei]

1226. ... Roses - `Розы [`rɒzy]

1227. ... Sunflowers - Под`солнухи [pʌt`sɒlnʊh'i]

1228. ... Tulips - Тюль`паны [t'ʊl"pʌny]

1229. ... Violets - Фи`алки [f'i`ʌlk'i]

1230. I need ... flowers - Мне `нужно ... [mn'e `nʊʒnʌ ...]

- After any numeral ending with 1 - except 11 - цве`ток [tsv'e`tɒk]

- After any numeral ending with 2, 3, 4 - except 12, 13, 14 - цвет`ка [tsv'et`kʌ]

- After the numerals 11-14 or any numeral ending with 0, 5, 6, 7, 8, 9 - цве`тов [tsv'et`kɒf]

See Numerals

1231. Do you want me to wrap them? - **Вам завернуть?** [vʌm zʌvʼerˋnʊtʼ]

1232. Wrap them just in plain paper please - **Заверˋните, поˋжалуйста, пˋросто в буˋмагу** [zʌvʼerˋnʼitʼe pʌˋʒalʊstʌ pˋrɒstʌ v bʊˋmʌgʊ]

1233. Wrap them in giftwrap please - **Заверˋните, поˋжалуйста, в поˋдарочную упаˋковку** [zʌvʼerˋnʼitʼe pʌˋʒalʊstʌ v pʌˋdʌrʌtʃnʊjʊ ʊpʌˋkɒfkʊ]

7.5. Buying Electronics and Householdware

1234. Where is the Electronics department? - **Где находится отˋдел электˋроники?** [gdʼe nʌˋhɒdʼitsʌ ʌtˋdʼel elʼekˋtrɒnʼikʼi]

1235. I would like to buy [a] ... - **Я хоˋчу куˋпить ...** [jʌ hʌˋtʃʊ kʊˋpʼitʼ ...]

1236. ... Batteries - **Батаˋрейки** [bʌtʌˋrʼejkʼi]

1237. ... Camera - **Фотоаппаˋрат** [fɒtʌpʌˋrʌt]

1238. ... Charger - **Заˋрядное устˋройство** [zʌˋrʼʌdnʌje ʊstˋrɒjstvʌ]

1239. ... Computer - **Комˋпьютер** [kʌmpˋjʊter]

1240. ... Headphones - **Наˋушники** [nʌˋʊʃnʼikʼi]

1241. ... Keyboard - **Клавиаˋтуру** [klʌvʼiʌˋtʊrʊ]

1242. ... Laptop - **Ноутˋбук** [nɒʊtˋbʊk]

1243. ... Mouse - **ˋМышку** [ˋmyʃkʊ]

1244. ... Printer - **Пˋринтер** [prʼinˋter]

1245. ... Smartphone - **Смартˋфон** [smartˋfɒn]

1246. ... Tablet - **Планˋшет** [plʌnˋʃet]

1247. I need to buy a power plug adapter can you recommend one to me? Here is my device – Мне `нужен а`даптер для ро`зеток, `можете мне `что-нибудь порекомендо`вать? Вот мо`ё уст`ройство [mn'e `nuʒen ʌ`dʌpter dl'ʌ rʌ`z'etʌk `mɒʒet'e mn'e `ʃtɒn'ibut' pʌr'ekʌm'endʌ `vʌt'? uɒt mʌ`jɒ ust`rɒjstvʌ]

1248. Have you got a ...? – У вас есть ...? [u vʌs jest' ...]

1249. ... Cup – К`ружка [k`ruʃkʌ]

1250. ... Extension cord – Удли`нитель [udl'i`n'it'el']

1251. ... Flashlight – Фо`нарик [fʌ`nʌr'ik]

1252. ... Fork – `Вилка [`v'ilkʌ]

1253. ... Frying pan – Сково`родка [skʌvʌ`rɒtkʌ]

1254. ... Glass (for water) – Ста`кан [stʌ`kʌn]

1255. ... Glass (for wine) – Бо`кал [bʌ`kʌl]

1256. ... Grater – `Тёрка [`t'ɒrkʌ]

1257. ... Hair dryer – Фен [f'en]

1258. ... Iron – У`тюг [ut'uk]

1259. ... Kettle – `Чайник [`tʃʌjn'ik]

1260. ... Knife – Нож [nɒʃ]

1261. ... Lamp – `Лампа [`lʌmpʌ]

1262. ... Light bulb – `Лампочка [lʌmpʌtʃ`kʌ]

1263. ... Plate – Та`релка [tʌ`r'elkʌ]

1264. ... Saucepan – Каст`рюля [kʌst`r'ul'ʌ]

1265. ... Spoon – `Ложка [`lɒʃkʌ]

1266. ... Teaspoon – `Чайная `ложка [`tʃʌjnʌjʌ `lɒʃkʌ]

1267. ... Water filter – `Фильтр для во`ды [f'il'tr dl'ʌ vʌ`dy]

7.6. Buying Medicine, Cosmetics, and Personal Hygiene Products

1268. I need ... - **Мне `нужно ку`пить** ... [mn'e `nuʒnʌ ku`p'it' ...]

1269. ... Aspirin - **Аспи`рин** [ʌsp'i`r'in]

1270. ... Condoms - **Презерва`тивы** [pr'ez'ervʌ`t'ivy]

1271. ... Contact lens solution - **`Жидкость для линз** [`ʒ'idkʌst' dl'ʌ `l'inz]

1272. ... Contact lenses - **Кон`тактные `линзы** [kʌn`tʌktnyje `l'inzy]

1273. ... Cotton bandage - **Бинт** [bint]

1274. ... Earplugs - **Бе`руши** [b'e`ruʃ'i]

1275. ... Laxatives - **Сла`бительное** [slʌ`b'it'el'nʌje]

1276. ... Medical patch - **П`ластырь** [p`lʌstyr']

1277. ... Painkillers - **Обез`боливающее** [ʌb'ez`bɒl'ivʌjuʃ'eje]

1278. ... Vitamins - **Вита`мины** [v'itʌ`m'iny]

1279. Do I need a prescription for this medicine? - **На `это лекарство `нужен ре`цепт?** [nʌ `etʌ le`kʌrstvʌ `nuʒen r'e`tsept]

1280. Have you got a prescription? - **У вас есть ре`цепт?** [u vʌs jest' r'e`tsept]

1281. This is prescription medicine only - **`Это ле`карство прода`ётся `только по ре`цепту** [`etʌ l'e`kʌrstvʌ prʌdʌ`jɒtsʌ `tɒl'kʌ pʌ r'e`tseptu]

1282. I need something for ... - **Мне `нужно ле`карство от** ... [mn'e `nuʒnʌ l'e`kʌrstvʌ ʌt ...]

1283. ... Allergy - **Аллер`гии** [ʌl'er`g'ii]

1284. ... Cold – **Прос`туды** [prʌs`tʊdy]

1285. ... Cough – **`Кашля** [`kʌʃl′ʌ]

1286. ... Diarrhea – **Диа`реи** [d′iʌ`rei]

1287. ... Flu – **Г`риппа** [g`r′ipʌ]

1288. ... Headache – **Голов`ной `боли** [gʌlʌv`nɒj `bɒl′i]

1289. ... Heartburn – **Из`жоги** [ɪz`ʒɒg′i]

1290. ... Running nose – **`Насморка** [`nʌsmʌrkʌ]

1291. ... Sore throat – **`Боли в `горле** [`bɒl′i v `gɒrl′e]

1292. ... Upset stomach – **Расст`ройства же`лудка** [rʌst`rɒjstvʌ ʒe`lʊtkʌ]

1293. There are some side-effects – **У `этого ле`карства есть по`бочные эф`фекты** [ʊ `etʌvʌ l′e`kʌrstvʌ jest′ pʌ`bɒtʃnyje e`f′ekty]

1294. There are no side-effects – **У `этого ле`карства нет поб`очных эф`фектов** [ʊ `etʌvʌ l′e`kʌrstvʌ n′et pʌ`bɒtʃnyh e`f′ektʌf]

1295. This medicine can make you a little drowsy / nauseous – **От `этого ле`карства `может быть сон`ливость / тошнота** [ɒt `etʌvʌ l′e`kʌrstvʌ `mɒʒet byt′ sʌn`l′ivʌst′ / tʌʃnʌ`tʌ]

1296. It is ... – **`Это ...** [`etʌ ...]

1297. ... Cream – **Крем** [kr′em]

1298. ... Drops – **`Капли** [`kʌpl′i]

1299. ... Ointment – **`Мазь** [mʌs′]

1300. ... Pills – **Таб`летки** [tʌb`l′etk′i]

1301. ... Syrup – **Си`роп** [s′i`rɒp]

1302. I want to buy ... - Я хо`чу ку`пить ... [jʌ hʌ`tʃʊ kʊ`p'it' ...]

1303. ... Cotton pads - `Ватные `диски [`vʌtnyje `d'isk'i]

1304. ... Cotton swabs - `Ватные `палочки [`vʌtnyje `pʌlʌtʃk'i]

1305. ... Deodorant - Дезодо`рант [dezdʌ`rʌnt]

1306. ... Face cream - Крем для ли`ца [kr'em dl'ʌ l'i`tsʌ]

1307. ... Liquid soap - `Жидкое `мыло [`ʒ'idkʌje `mylʌ]

1308. ... Hair brush - Рас`чёску [rʌ`ʃ"ʊskʊ]

1309. ... Paper tissues - Сал`фетки [sʌl`f'etk'i]

1310. ... Perfume - Ду`хи [dʊ`h'i]

1311. ... Shampoo - Шам`пунь [ʃʌm`pʊn']

1312. ... Shower gel - Гель для `душа [g'el' dl'ʌ `dʊʃʌ]

1313. ... Soap - `Мыло [`mylʌ]

1314. ... Toilet paper - Туа`летную бу`магу [tʊʌ`l'etnʊjʊ bʊ`mʌgʊ]

1315. ... Toothbrush - Зуб`ную `щётку [zʊb`nʊjʊ `ʃ"ʊtkʊ]

1316. ... Toothpaste - Зуб`ную `пасту [zʊb`nʊjʊ `pʌstʊ]

1317. ... Shaving foam - `Пену для бри`тья [`p'enʊ dl'ʌ br'it'jʌ]

1318. ... Shaving gel - Гель для бри`тья [g'el' dl'ʌ br'it'jʌ]

1319. ... Shaving razor - Б`ритву [b`r'itvʊ]

Chapter 8. Accommodation, Eating and Services

8.1. Hotels, Hostels and Flats

1320. Can you recommend any good hotels? - `Можете порекомендо`вать хо`рошие о`тели? [`mɒʒet'e r'ekʌm'endʌ`vʌt' kʌ`k'ijen'ibʊt' hʌ`rɒʃije ʌ`tel'i]

1321. How many stars has the hotel got? - С`колько у `этого отеля звёзд? [s`kɒl'kʌ ʊ `etʌvʌ ʌ`tel'ʌ z`v'ɒst]

1322. I'd like to stay in a ... - Мне бы хо`телось остано`виться в ... [mn'e by hʌ`t'elʌs' ʌstʌnʌ`v'itsʌ v ...]

1323. ... Flat - Квар`тире [kvʌr`t'ir'e]

1324. ... Hotel - Гос`тинице [gʌs`t'in'itse]

1325. ... Hostel - `Хостеле [`hɒstel'e]

1326. How far is it from the city center / railway station / airport? - Как дале`ко он от `центра / вок`зала / аэропор`та? [kʌk dʌl'e`kɒ ɒn ʌt `tsentrʌ / vʌk`zʌlʌ / ʌerʌpʌr`tʌ]

1327. Are there any vacancies? - У вас есть сво`бодные мес`та? [ʊ vʌs jest' svʌ`bɒdnyje m'es`tʌ]

1328. No vacancies - Мест нет [m'est n'et]

1329. I'd like a ... - Мне `нужен ... [mn'e `nʊʒen ...]

1330. ... Single room - Одно`местный `номер [ʌdnʌ`m'esnyj `nɒm'er]

1331. ... Double room - Двух`местный `номер с од`ной кро`ватью [dvʊh`m'esnyj `nɒm'er s ʌd`nɒj krʌ`vʌt'jʊ]

1332. ... Twin room – Двух`местный `номер с дву`мя кро`ватями [dvuh`m'esnyj `nɒm'er s dvu`m'ʌ krʌ`vʌt'ʌm'i]

1333. Is there (a/an) ... in the room? – В `комнате есть ...? [v `kɒmnʌt'e jest' ...]

1334. ... Bathroom – `Ванная [`vʌnʌjʌ]

1335. ... Balcony – Бал`кон [bʌl`kɒn]

1336. ... Air-conditioning – Кондицио`нер [kʌnd'its'iʌ`n'er]

1337. ... Fridge – Холо`дильник [hʌlʌ`d'il'n'ik]

1338. ... Internet access – Интер`нет [ınter`net]

1339. ... Safe – Сейф [s'ejf]

1340. ... Telephone – Теле`фон [t'el'e`fɒn]

1341. ... TV – Теле`визор [t'el'e`v'izʌr]

1342. I need (a/an) ... – Мне нуж`но ... [mn'e `nuʒnʌ ...]

1343. ... Child's bed – `Детская кро`вать [`d'etskʌjʌ krʌ`vʌt']

1344. ... Extra bed – Допол`нительная кро`вать [dʌpʌl`n'it'el'nʌjʌ krʌ`vʌt']

1345. ... Extra blanket – Допол`нительное оде`яло [dʌpʌl`n'it'el'nʌje ʌd'ejʌlʌ]

1346. ... Iron – У`тюг [ut'uk]

1347. ... Laundry service – П`рачечная [p`rʌtʃ'etʃnʌjʌ]

1348. How do I access the Internet? – Как полу`чить `доступ к интер`нету? [kʌk pɒlutʃ'it' dɒstup k 'int'ern'etu]

1349. Is there free Wi-Fi? – Тут есть бесп`латный вай-фай? [tut jest' b'esp`lʌtnyj vʌjfʌj]

1350. What is the Wi-Fi password? – **Какой па`роль для вай-фая?** [kʌ`kɒj pʌ`rɒlʲ dlʲʌ vʌjfʌjʌ]

1351. Is there a swimming pool / gym? – **У вас есть бас`сейн / трена`жёрный зал?** [ʊ vʌs jestʲ bʌ`sʲejn / trʲenʌ`ʒɒrnyj zʌl]

1352. Do you allow pets? – **У вас `можно с жи`вотными?** [ʊ vʌs `mɒʒnʌ s ʒʲi`vɒtnymʲi]

1353. Do you have a car park? – **У вас есть пар`ковка?** [ʊ vʌs jestʲ pʌr`kɒfkʌ]

1354. What is the price per night? – **Ка`кая це`на за од`ну ночь?** [kʌ`kʌjʌ tse`nʌ zʌ ʌd`nʊ nɒtʃ]

1355. Have you got cheaper rooms? – **У вас есть `более де`шёвые номе`ра?** [ʊ vʌs jestʲ `bɒlʲeje dʲe`ʃɒvyje nʌmʲe`rʌ]

1356. What is the total? – **Ка`кая и`тоговая `сумма?** [kʌ`kʌjʌ i`tɒgʌvʌjʌ `sʊmʌ]

1357. Is breakfast included? – **Вклю`чён ли `завтрак?** [ʊklʲʊ`tʃɒn lʲi `zʌvtrʌk]

1358. Is it a full-board or a half-board? – **`Это панси`он или `полупансион?** [`etʌ pʌnsʲi`ɒn ilʲi `pɒlʊpʌnsʲi`ɒn]

1359. Is there a transfer to the airport? – **Есть ли у вас транс`фер в аэро`порт?** [jestʲ lʲi ʊ vʌs trʌns`fʲer v ʌerʌ`pɒrt]

1360. Could I see the room? – **`Можно посмот`реть `номер?** [`mɒʒnʌ pʌsmʌt`retʲ `nɒmʲer]

1361. I would like to make a room reservation – **Я хо`чу забро`нировать `номер** [jʌ hʌ`tʃʊ zʌbrʌ`nʲirʌvʌtʲ `nɒmʲer]

1362. I would like to check in – **Я хо`чу зарегист`рироваться** [jʌ hʌ`tʃʊ zʌrʲegʲistʲ`rʲirʌvʌtsʌ]

1363. I have got a reservation - У ме`ня забро`нировано [ʋ m'e`n'ʌ zʌbrʌ`n'irʌvʌnʌ]

1364. What time is the breakfast / lunch / dinner? - Во с`колько `завтрак / о`бед / `ужин? [vʌ s`kɒl'kʌ `zʌvtrʌk / ʌ`b'et / ʋ`ʒin]

1365. Could I have breakfast in my room? - `Можно зака`зать `завтрак в `номер? [`mɒʒnʌ zʌkʌ`zʌt' `zʌvtrʌk v `nɒm'er]

1366. What time does the bar close? - Во с`колько закры`вается бар? [vʌ s`kɒl'kʌ zʌkry`vʌjetsʌ bʌr]

1367. Where is the lift? - Где лифт? [gd'e l'ift]

1368. Could I have a wake-up call at …? - `Можете разбу`дить ме`ня в …? [`mɒʒet'e rʌzbʋ`d'it' m'e`n'ʌ v …]

See **Numerals** and **Time**

1369. Could you please call me a taxi? - `Вызовите мне, по`жалуйста, так`си [vyzʌv'i`t'e mn'e pʌ`ʒʌlʋstʌ tʌk`s'i]

1370. What time is the check-out? - Во с`колько `нужно `выехать? [ʋʌ s`kɒl'kʌ `nʋʒnʌ `vyjehʌt']

1371. Could you clean my room please - Убе`рите, по`жалуйста, мо`ю `комнату [ʋb'e`r'it'e pʌ`ʒʌlʋstʌ mʌ`jʋ `kɒmnʌtʋ]

1372. Do not disturb please - Не беспо`коить, по`жалуйста [n'e b'espʌ``kɒ'it' pʌ`ʒʌlʋstʌ]

1373. Change my sheets please - Поме`няйте мне, по`жалуйста, пос`тельное бе`льё [pʌm'e`n'ʌjt'e mn'e pʌ`ʒʌlʋstʌ pʌs`t'el'nʌje b'e`l'jɒ]

1374. My room has not been made up - Моя `комната не п`рибрана [mʌ`jʌ `kɒmnʌtʌ n'e p`r'ibrʌnʌ]

1375. Who is there? – **Кто там?** [ktɒ tʌm]

1376. I have lost my room key – **Я поте`рял** (masculine) / **поте`ряла** (feminine) **ключ от `номера** [jʌ pʌt'e`r'ʌl / pʌt'e`r'ʌlʌ klutʃ ʌt `nɒm'erʌ]

1377. There is not any hot water in my room – **У ме`ня в `номере нет го`рячей во`ды** [u m'e`n'ʌ v `nɒm'er'e n'et gʌ`r'ʌtʃej vʌ`dy]

1378. It is very cold in my room – **В мо`ём `номере `очень `холодно** [u mʌ`jɒm `nɒm'ere `ɒtʃen' hɒlʌdnʌ]

1379. There are problems with the ... in my room – **У ме`ня в `номере проб`лемы с ...** [u m'e`n'ʌ v `nɒm'ere prʌb`l'emy s ...]

1380. ... Air-conditioning – **Кондицио`нером** [kʌnd'its'iʌ`n'erʌm]

1381. ... Electricity – **Элект`ричеством** [el'ekt`r'itʃestvʌm]

1382. ... Fridge – **Холо`дильником** [hʌlʌ`d'il'n'ikʌm]

1383. ... Safe – **`Сейфом** [`sejfʌm]

1384. ... Shower – **`Душем** [`duʃem]

1385. ... TV – **Теле`визором** [t'el'e`v'izʌrʌm]

1386. Could you call someone to fix it – **Позовите, по`жалуйста, ко`го-нибудь `это почи`нить** [pʌzʌ`v'it'e pʌ`ʒʌlustʌ kʌ`vɒn'ibut' `etʌ pʌtʃ'i`n'it']

1387. There is no ... in my room – **У ме`ня в `номере нет ...** [u m'e`n'ʌ v `nɒm'ere n'et ...]

1388. ... Bed sheets – **Пос`тельного бе`лья** [pʌs`t'el'nʌvʌ b'el'jʌ]

1389. ... Soap – **`Мыла** [`mylʌ]

1390. ... Shampoo – **Шам`пуня** [ʃʌm`pun'ʌ]

1391. ... Towel - Поло`тенца [pʌlʌ`t'entsʌ]

1392. ... Water - Во`ды [ʊʌ`dy]

1393. Are there any messages for me? - Мне не остав`ляли сооб`щений? [mn'e n'e ʌstʌv`lʌl'i sʌb`ʃ'en'ij]

1394. I would like to check out - Я хо`чу `выехать [jʌ hʌ`tʃʊ `vyjehʌt']

1395. I would like to pay my bill - Я хо`чу опла`тить счёт [jʌ hʌ`tʃʊ ʌplʌ`t'it' ʃ'ɒt]

1396. Can I leave my luggage here for several hours? - `Можно ост`авить у вас ба`гаж на нес`колько ча`сов? [`mɒʒnʌ ʌs`tʌv'it' ʊ vʌs bʌ`gʌʒ nʌ `n'eskʌl'kʌ tʃʌ`sɒf]

1397. Could I have some help with the luggage? - Помо`гите, по`жалуйста, с бага`жом [pʌmʌ`g'it'e pʌ`ʒʌlʊstʌ s bʌgʌ`ʒɒm]

1398. What kind of rooms are there in your hostel? - Какие `комнаты есть в `вашем `хостеле? [kʌ`k'ie `kɒmnʌty jest' v `vʌʃem `hɒstel'e]

1399. How many people are there in the room? - С`колько чело`век в од`ной `комнате? [s`kɒl'kʌ tʃ'elʌ`v'ek v ʌd`nɒj `kɒmnʌt'e]

1400. Is there a shower within the room or a shared one on the floor? - Душ в `комнате или на эта`же? [dʊʃ v `kɒmnʌt'e il'i nʌ etʌ`ʒe]

1401. Is there a kitchen? - Есть ли `кухня? [jest' l'i `kʊhn'ʌ]

1402. Are there any lockers? - Есть ли ш`кафчики для ве`щей? [jest' l'i ʃ`kʌftʃ'ik'i dl'ʌ v'e`ʃ'ej]

1403. Could you be a little quieter, please? - По`жалуйста, не шу`мите [pʌ`ʒʌlʊstʌ n'e ʃʊ`m'it'e]

1404. May I turn the light off / on? – `Можно `выключить / вклю`чить свет? [`mɒʒnʌ `vykl'ʊtʃ'it' / vkl'ʊ`tʃ'it' sv'et]

1405. Where are the sockets? – Где на`ходятся ро`зетки? [gd'e nʌ`hɒd'ʌtsʌ rʌ`z'etk'i]

1406. I want to rent a flat – Я хо`чу снять квар`тиру [jʌ hʌ`tʃʊ sn'ʌt' kvʌr`t'irʊ]

1407. Can I rent daily? – `Можно сни`мать по`суточно? [`mɒʒnʌ sn'i`mʌt' pʌ`sʊtʌtʃnʌ]

1408. Can I rent for … days? – `Можно снять на …? [`mɒʒnʌ snʌt' nʌ …]

   – After any numeral ending with 1 – except 11 – день [den']

   – After any numeral ending with 2, 3, 4 – except 12, 13, 14 – дня [dn'ʌ]

   – After the numerals 11-14 or any numeral ending with 0, 5, 6, 7, 8, 9 – дней [dn'ej]

See Numerals

1409. Which floor is the flat on? – На ка`ком эта`же квар`тира? [nʌ kʌ`kɒm etʌ`ʒe kvʌr`t'irʌ]

1410. The flat is on the first / second / third / forth / … floor – Квар`тира на `первом / вто`ром / т`ретьем / чет`вёртом / … этаже [kvʌr`t'irʌ nʌ `p'ervʌm / vtʌ`rɒm / t`ret'jem / tʃet`v'ɒrtʌm / … `etʌʒe]

See Numerals

1411. Can I get another set of keys? – `Можно полу`чить е`щё од`ни клю`чи? [`mɒʒnʌ pʌlʊ`tʃ'it' eʃ'ɒ ʌd`ni klʊ`tʃi]

8.2. Food and Restaurants

1412. What cuisine do you prefer? - **Ка`кую `кухню вы предпочи`таете** (polite / plural) **/ ты предпочи`таешь?** (informal) [kʌ`kuju `kuhn'u vy pr'etpʌtʃ'i`tʌjet'e / ty pr'etpʌtʃ'i`tʌjeʃ]

1413. I would prefer ... cuisine - **Я предпочи`таю ... `кухню** [jʌ pr'edpʌtʃ'i`tʌju ... `kuhn'u]

1414. ... Asian - **ази`атскую** [ʌz'i`ʌtskuju]

1415. ... Chinese - **ки`тайскую** [k'i`tʌjskuju]

1416. ... European - **евро`пейскую** [jevrʌ`p'ejskuju]

1417. ... French - **фран`цузскую** [frʌn`tsuzskuju]

1418. ... Italian - **ита`льянскую** [itʌl''jʌnskuju]

1419. ... Japanese - **я`понскую** [jʌ`pɒnskuju]

1420. ... Russian - **`русскую** [`ruskuju]

1421. What kind of dishes do you like? - **Ка`кие б`люда вам** (polite / plural) **/ те`бе** (informal) **н`равятся?** [kʌ`k'ie b`l'udʌ vʌm / t'e`b'e n`rʌv'ʌtsʌ]

1422. Do you want to have breakfast / lunch / dinner? - **Хо`тите** (polite / plural) **/ `Хочешь** (informal) **по`завтракать / поо`бедать / по`ужинать?** [hʌ`t'it'e / `hɒtʃ'eʃ pʌ`zʌvftrʌkʌt' / pʌʌ`b'edʌt' / pʌ`uʒinʌt']

1423. Do you want to taste it? - **Хотите** (polite / plural) **/ Хочешь** (informal) **попробовать?** [hʌ`t'it'e / `hɒtʃ'eʃ pʌp`rɒbʌvʌt']

1424. It smells good - **В`кусно `пахнет!** [f`kusnʌ `pʌhn'et]

1425. It tastes good - **В`кусно!** [f`kusnʌ]

1426. Do you have any free tables? - **У вас есть сво`бодные с`толики?** [ʊ vʌs jest' svʌ`bɒdnyje s`tɒl'ik'i]

1427. I need a table for ... people - **`Нужен с`толик на ...** [`nʊʒen s`tɒl'ik nʌ ...]

- After any numeral ending with 1 - except 11 - **чело`века** [tʃ'elʌ`v'ek]

- After any numeral ending with 2, 3, 4 - except 12, 13, 14 - **чело`века** [tʃ'elʌ`v'ekʌ]

- After the numerals 11-14 or any numeral ending with 0, 5, 6, 7, 8, 9 - **чело`век** [tʃ'elʌ`v'ek]

See Numerals

1428. Your table will be ready in just a moment - **Ваш с`толик сей`час `будет го`тов** [vʌʃ s`tɒl'ik sej`tʃʌs `bʊd'et gʌ`tɒf]

1429. Where can I leave my jacket / coat? - **Где `можно ос`тавить `верхнюю о`дежду?** [gd'e `mɒʒnʌ ʌs`tʌv'it' `v'erhn'ujʊ ʌ`d'eʒdʊ]

1430. Where is the toilet? - **Где у вас туа`лет?** [gd'e ʊ vʌs tʊʌ`l'et]

1431. I need a waiter - **Мне `нужен офици`ант** [mn'e `nʊʒen ʌf'i`tsʌnt]

1432. Can I make an order now? - **`Можно с`делать за`каз?** [`mɒʒnʌ s`d'elʌt' zʌ`kʌz]

1433. What is today's special? - **Ка`кое у вас се`годня б`людо дня?** [kʌ`kɒje ʊ vʌs s'e`vɒdn'ʌ b`l'ʊdʌ dn'ʌ]

1434. Could you clean the table, please? - **`Вытрите, по`жалуйста, стол** [`vytr'it'e pʌ`ʒʌlʊstʌ stɒl]

1435. Give me a menu please - **`Дайте, по`жалуйста, ме`ню** [`dʌjt'e pʌ`ʒʌlʊstʌ m'e`n'ʊ]

1436. Have you got a menu in English? – **У вас есть ме`ню на анг`лийском?** [u vʌs jest' mʲeˈnʲu nʌ ʌngˈlʲskʌm]

1437. Do you have a high chair for a child? – **У вас есть `детский с`тульчик?** [u vʌs jest' `dʲetskʲij sˈtulʲtʃʲik]

1438. Are you ready to order? – **Вы го`товы за`казывать?** [vy gʌˈtɒvy zʌˈkʌzyvʌtʲ]

1439. I am not ready yet – **Я е`щё не го`тов** (masculine) / **го`това** (feminine) [jʌ eˈʃʲɒ nʲe gʌˈtɒf / gʌˈtɒvʌ]

1440. Yes, I am ready to order – **Да, я го`тов** (masculine) / **го`това** (feminine) **за`казывать** [dʌ jʌ gʌˈtɒf / gʌˈtɒvʌ zʌˈkʌzyvʌtʲ]

1441. What are your specialties? – **Ка`кие у вас `фирменные б`люда?** [kʌˈkʲie u vʌs ˈfʲirmʲenyje bˈlʲudʌ]

1442. What would you like to drink? – **Что `будете пить?** [ʃtɒ ˈbudʲetʲe pʲitʲ]

1443. Could I see the wine list, please? – **`Дайте, по`жалуйста, `винную `карту** [ˈdʌjtʲe pʌˈʒʌlustʌ ˈvʲinuju ˈkʌrtu]

1444. I will take (a/an) ... – **Я возь`му ...** [jʌ vʌzʲˈmu ...]

1445. ... Appetizers – **За`куски** [zʌˈkuskʲi]

1446. ... Main course – **Вто`рое б`людо** [vtʌˈrɒje bˈlʲudʌ]

1447. ... Side dish – **Гар`нир** [gʌrˈnʲir]

1448. ... Dessert – **Де`серт** [dʲeˈsʲert]

1449. ... Set-menu – **`Бизнес-ланч** [ˈbʲiznʲeslʌntʃ]

1450. I would like my steak rare / medium / well-done – **Мне `нужен с`лабо про`жаренный / с`редне про`жаренный / хоро`шо про`жаренный стейк**

[mn'e `nuʒen s`lʌbʌ prʌ`ʒʌr'enyj / s`r'edn'e prʌ`ʒʌr'enyj / hʌrʌ`ʃɒ prʌ`ʒʌr'enyj st'ejk]

1451. Is this a …? - `Это … [`etʌ …]

1452. … Baked dish - **Пе`чёное** [p'e`ʧ"ɒnʌje]

1453. … Boiled dish - **Ва`рёное** [vʌ`r'ɒnʌje]

1454. … Fried dish - **`Жареное** [`ʒʌr'enʌje]

1455. … Grilled dish - **Б`людо на г`риле** [b`l'udʌ nʌ gr'il'e]

1456. … Salad - **Са`лат** [sʌ`lʌt]

1457. … Soup - **Суп** [sup]

1458. … Stew - **Ту`шёное** [tu`ʃɒnʌje]

1459. Do you have any vegetarian food? - **У вас есть вегетарианские блюда?** [u vʌs jest' v'eg`etʌr'i`ʌnsk'ije b`l'udʌ]

1460. How long do I have to wait? - **С`колько мне ж`дать?** [s`kɒl'kʌ mn'e ʒdʌt']

1461. Is it spicy? - **`Это `острое?** [`etʌ `ɒstrʌje]

1462. Bon appetite - **При`ятного аппе`тита!** [pr'i`jʌtnʌvʌ ʌp'e`t'itʌ]

1463. Could you bring … please? - **Прине`сите, по`жалуйста,** … [pr'in'e`s'it'e pʌ`ʒʌlustʌ …]

1464. … Bread - **Хлеб** [hl'ep]

1465. … Oil - **Рас`тительное `масло** [rʌs`t'it'el'nʌje `mʌslʌ]

1466. … Napkins - **Сал`фетки** [sʌl`f'etk'i]

1467. … Pepper - **`Перец** [`p'er'ets]

1468. … Salt - **Соль** [sɒl']

1469. … Sugar - **Сахар** [`sʌhʌr]

1470. ... Toothpicks – **Зубо`чистки** [zʊbʌ`tʃ'istk'i]

1471. This is not what I ordered – **Я не `это за`казывал** (masculine) **/ за`казывала** (feminine) [jʌ n'e `etʌ zʌ`kʌzyvʌl / zʌ`kʌzyvʌlʌ]

1472. Can I see the manager, please? – **Я хо`чу у`видеть `менеджера** [jʌ hʌ`tʃʊ ʊ`v'idet' `menedʒerʌ]

1473. This dish tastes strange – **У `этого блюда ст`ранный вкус** [ʊ `etʌvʌ b`l'ʊdʌ st`rʌnyj fkʊs]

1474. It is not fresh – **Нес`вежее!** [n'es`v'eʒeje]

1475. It is too spicy / salty – **С`лишком `остро / со`лёно** [ʃ`l'iʃkʌm `ɒstrʌ / sʌ`l'ɒnʌ]

1476. Can I have a bill, please – **Прине`сите мне чек, по`жалуйста** [pr'in'e`s'it'e mn'e tʃek pʌ`ʒʌlʊstʌ]

1477. Can we have a split bill please? – **`Можно нам посчи`тать от`дельно?** [`mɒʒnʌ nʌm pʌʌʃ'i`tʌt' ʌt`d'el'nʌ]

1478. Could you check the bill, please? It does not seem right – **Про`верьте, по`жалуйста, чек, тут ка`кая-то о`шибка** [prʌ`v'er'ť'e pʌ`ʒʌlʊstʌ tʃek tʊt kʌ`kʌjʌtʌ ʌ`ʃ'ipkʌ]

1479. Thank you, it was delicious – **Спа`сибо, `было `очень в`кусно** [ʃpʌs'ibʌ `bylʌ `ɒtʃen' v`kʊsnʌ]

1480. Can I get this to-go? – **`Можно `это упако`вать мне с со`бой?** [`mɒʒnʌ `etʌ ʊpʌkʌ`vʌt' mn'e s sʌ`bɒj]

1481. How much do they usually tip? – **С`колько о`бычно остав`ляют чае`вые?** [s`kɒl'kʌ ʌ`bytʃnʌ ʌstʌv`l'ʌjʊt tʃʌje`vyje]

1482. What kind of fruit is this? – **Что `это за фрукт?** [ʃtɒ `etʌ zʌ frʊkt]

1483. This is a / an ... – **`Это ...** [`etʌ ...]

1484. ... Apple - `Яблоко [`jʌblʌkʌ]

1485. ... Apricot - Абри`кос [ʌbr'i`kɒs]

1486. ... Banana - Ба`нан [bʌ`nʌn]

1487. ... Blueberry - Чер`ника [tʃ'er`n'ikʌ]

1488. ... Cherry - `Вишня [`v'iʃn'ʌ]

1489. ... Grapefruit - Грейп`фрут [grejp`frʊt]

1490. ... Grapes - Виног`рад [v'inʌg`rʌt]

1491. ... Lemon - Ли`мон [l'i`mɒn]

1492. ... Lime - `Лайм [lʌjm]

1493. ... Mango - `Манго [`mʌngʌ]

1494. ... Melon - `Дыня [`dyn'ʌ]

1495. ... Orange - Апель`син [ʌp'el'`s'in]

1496. ... Peach - `Персик [`p'ers'ik]

1497. ... Pear - Г`руша [g`rʊʃʌ]

1498. ... Pineapple - Ана`нас [ʌnʌ`nʌs]

1499. ... Plum - С`лива [s`l'ivʌ]

1500. ... Raspberry - Ма`лина [mʌ`l'inʌ]

1501. ... Strawberry - Клуб`ника [klʊb`n'ikʌ]

1502. ... Watermelon - Ар`буз [ʌr`bʊs]

1503. What kind of vegetable is it? - Какой `это овощ? [kʌ`kɒj `etʌ `ɒvʌʃ']

1504. This is ... - `Это ... [`etʌ ...]

1505. ... Aubergine - Бакла`жан [bʌklʌ`ʒʌn]

1506. ... Avocado - Аво`кадо [ʌvʌ`kʌdʌ]

1507. ... Beans - Фа`соль [fʌ`sɒl']

1508. ... Beetroot - С`вёкла [ʃ`v'ɒklʌ]

1509. ... Bell pepper - Бол`гарский `перец [bʌl`gʌrsk'ij `p'er'ets]

1510. ... Broccoli - Б`рокколи [b`rɒkʌl'i]

1511. ... Cabbage - Ка`пуста [kʌ`pʊstʌ]

1512. ... Carrot - Мор`ковь [mʌr`kɒf']

1513. ... Cauliflower - Цвет`ная ка`пуста [tʃv´et`nʌjʌ kʌ`pʊstʌ]

1514. ... Celery - Сельде`рей [s'el'd'e`r'ej]

1515. ... Cucumber - Огу`рец [ʌgʊ`r'ets]

1516. ... Garlic - Чес`нок [tʃ'es`nɒk]

1517. ... Lettuce - Са`лат [sʌ`lʌt]

1518. ... Mushrooms - Гри`бы [gr'i`by]

1519. ... Onion - Лук [lʊk]

1520. ... Peas - Го`рох [gʌ`rɒh]

1521. ... Potato - Кар`тофель / Кар`тошка [kʌr`tɒfel' / kʌr`tɒʃkʌ]

1522. ... Pumpkin - `Тыква [`tykvʌ]

1523. ... Spinach - Шпи`нат [ʃp'i`nʌt]

1524. ... Tomato - Поми`дор [pʌm'i`dɒr]

1525. ... Zucchini - Цук`кини [tʃʊ`k'in'i]

1526. Are there any nuts in this dish? - В `этом б`люде есть о`рехи? [u `etʌm b`l'ʊde jest' ʌ`r'eh'i]

1527. What kind of nuts are they? - Ка`кие `это о`рехи? [kʌ`k'ie `etʌ ʌ`r'eh'i]

1528. This is ... - `Это ... [`etʌ ...]

1529. ... Almond - Мин`даль [m'in`dʌl']

1530. ... Cashew - `Кешью [`k'eʃjʊ]

1531. ... Coconut - **Ко`кос** [kʌ`kɒs]

1532. ... Peanut - **А`рахис** [ʌ`rʌh'is]

1533. ... Pistachio - **Фис`ташки** [f'is`tʌʃk'i]

1534. ... Walnut - **Г`рецкий о`рех** [gr'etsk'ij ʌ`r'eh]

1535. What kind of grain is it? - **Какая `это крупа?** [kʌ`kʌjʌ `etʌ krʊ`pʌ]

1536. This is ... - **`Это ...** [`etʌ ...]

1537. ... Buckwheat - **Г`речка** [g`r'etʃkʌ]

1538. ... Lentils - **Чече`вица** [tʃ'etʃ'e`v'itsʌ]

1539. ... Millet - **Пше`но** [pʃe`nɒ]

1540. ... Oatmeal - **Ов`сянка** [ʌf`s'ʌnkʌ]

1541. ... Rice - **Рис** [r'is]

1542. What kind of meat is it? - **Какое `это мясо?** [kʌ`kɒje `etʌ `m'ʌsʌ]

1543. It is ... - **`Это ...** [`etʌ ...]

1544. ... Bacon - **Бе`кон** [b'e`kɒn]

1545. ... Beef - **Го`вядина** [gʌ`v'ʌd'inʌ]

1546. ... Chicken - **`Курица** [`kʊr'itsʌ]

1547. ... Duck - **`Утка** [`ʊtkʌ]

1548. ... Lamb - **Яг`нёнок** [jʌg`n'ɒnʌk]

1549. ... Mutton - **Ба`ранина** [bʌ`rʌn'inʌ]

1550. ... Pork - **Сви`нина** [sv'i`n'inʌ]

1551. ... Rabbit - **К`ролик** [k`rɒl'ik]

1552. ... Turkey - **Ин`дейка** [ɪn`d'ejkʌ]

1553. What kind of fish or seafood is it? - **Ка`кая `это `рыба `или морепро`дукты?** [kʌ`kʌjʌ `etʌ `rybʌ il'i mʌr'eprʌ`dʊkty]

1554. It is … – `Это … [`etʌ …]

1555. … Caviar – Ик`ра [ɪk`rʌ]

1556. … Cod – Трес`ка [tr′es`kʌ]

1557. … Crab – Краб [krʌp]

1558. … Crayfish – Рак [rʌk]

1559. … Eel – `Угорь [`ʊgʌr′]

1560. … Lobster – `Лобстер [`lɒpster]

1561. … Mussels – `Мидии [`m′id′ii]

1562. … Octopus – Осьми`ног [ʌs′m′i`nɒk]

1563. … Oysters – `Устрицы [`ʊstr′itsy]

1564. … Prawn – Тиг`ровая кре`ветка [t′ig`rɒvʌjʌ kr′e`v′etkʌ]

1565. … Salmon – Ло`сось [lʌ`sɒs′]

1566. … Sardines – Сар`дины [sʌrd′iny]

1567. … Scallop – Гребе`шок [gr′eb′e`ʃɒk]

1568. … Shrimps – Кре`ветки [kr′e`v′etk′i]

1569. … Squid – Каль`мар [kʌl′`mʌr]

1570. … Trout – Фо`рель [fʌ`rel′]

1571. … Tuna – Ту`нец [tʊ`n′ets]

1572. What kind of desserts have you got? – Ка`кие у вас есть де`серты? [kʌ`k′ije ʊ vʌs jest′ d′e`s′erty]

1573. We have got … – У нас есть … [ʊ nʌs jest′ …]

1574. … Biscuits – Пе`ченье [p′e`tʃ′en′e]

1575. … Brownies – Б`рауни [b`rʌʊn′i]

1576. … Buns – `Булочка [`bʊlʌtʃkʌ]

1577. … Cakes – Пи`рожные [p′i`rɒʒnyje]

1578. ... Chocolate - **Шоко`лад** [ʃʌkʌ`lʌt]

1579. ... Croissants - **Круас`саны** [krʊʌ`sʌny]

1580. ... Cupcakes - **`Кексы** [`k'eksy]

1581. ... Éclairs - **Эк`леры** [ek`l'ery]

1582. ... Fruit tarts - **Фрук`товые кор`зиночки** [frʊk`tɒvyje kʌr`z'inʌtʃk'i]

1583. ... Ice-cream - **Мо`роженое** [mʌ`rɒʒenʌje]

1584. ... Jelly - **Же`ле** [ʒe`l'e]

1585. ... Mousse - **Мусс** [mʊs]

1586. ... Pancakes - **Бли`ны** [bl'i`ny]

1587. ... Pastry - **`Выпечка** [`vyp'etʃkʌ]

1588. ... Pies - **Пиро`ги** [p'irʌ`g'i]

(Note that the word **пирог** in Russian can describe very different kinds of pastries - closed ones, open ones, big ones, and small ones.)

1589. ... Soufflé - **Суф`ле** [ʃʊf`l'e]

1590. ... Strudels - **Шт`рудель** [ʃt`rʊd'el']

1591. ... Vatrushkas - **Ват`рушки** [vʌt`rʊʃk'i]

(**Ват`рушка** is a kind of pastry typical for Russian cuisine - an open pie filled with cottage cheese.)

1592. Are there any dairy products in here? - **Здесь есть мо`лочные про`дукты?** [zd'es' jest' mʌ`lɒtʃnyje prʌ`dʊkty]

1593. Is / are there any ... in here? - **Здесь есть ...?** [zd'es' jest' ...]

1594. ... Eggs - **`Яйца** [`jʌjtsʌ]

1595. ... Fish - **`Рыба** [`rybʌ]

1596. ... Honey - **Мёд** [m'ɒt]

1597. ... Milk - Моло`ко [mʌlʌ`kɒ]

1598. ... Meat - `Мясо [`m'ʌsʌ]

1599. ... Wheat - Пше`ница [pʃe`n'itsʌ]

1600. What kind of dairy product is it? - Какой `это мо`лочный про`дукт? [kʌ`kɒj ``etʌ mʌ`lɒtʃnyj prʌ`dʊkt]

1601. This is ... - `Это ... [`etʌ ...]

1602. ... Butter - С`ливочное `масло [s`l'ivʌtʃnʌje `mʌslʌ]

1603. ... Cheese - Сыр [syr]

1604. ... Cottage cheese - Тво`рог [tvʌ`rɒk]

1605. ... Cream - С`ливки [s`l'ifk'i]

1606. ... Kefir - Ке`фир [k'e`f'ir]

(Кефир is a dairy product typical for Russian cuisine - a fermented milk drink a bit similar to plain thin yoghurt.)

1607. ... Milk - Моло`ко [mʌlʌ`kɒ]

1608. ... Sour cream - Сме`тана [sm'e`tʌnʌ]

1609. ... Yoghurt - `Йогурт [`jɒgʊrt]

1610. What kind of non-alcoholic beverages have you got? - Ка`кие у вас есть безалко`гольные на`питки? [kʌ`k'ie ʊ vʌs jest' b'ezʌlkʌ`gɒl'nyje nʌ`p'itk'i]

1611. We have got ... - У нас есть ... [ʊ nʌs jest' ...]

1612. ... Black / Green / Herbal tea - `Чёрный / Зе`лёный / Травя`ной чай [`tʃɒrnyj / z'e`l'ɒnyj / trʌv'ʌ`nɒj tʃʌj]

1613. ... Coffee - `Кофе [`kɒf'e]

1614. ... Fresh juice - Свеже`выжатый сок [sv'eʒe`vyʒʌtyj sɒk]

1615. ... Juice - **Сок** [sɒk]

1616. ... Kvas - **Квас** [kvʌs]

(**Квас** is a traditional Russian drink made of fermented bread.)

1617. ... Lemonade - **Лимо`над** [l'imʌ`nʌd]

1618. ... Milk shake - **Мо`лочный кок`тейль** [mʌ`lɒtʃnyj kʌk`tejl']

1619. ... Mineral water - **Мине`ральная во`да** [m'in'e`rʌl'nʌjʌ vʌ`dʌ]

1620. ... Smoothie - **С`музи** [s`mʊz'i]

1621. ... Soft drinks - **Прохла`дительные на`питки** [prʌhlʌ`d'it'el'nyje nʌ`p'itk'i]

1622. Do you want still water? - **Вам без `газа?** [vʌm b'ez `gʌzʌ]

1623. Do you want sparkling water? - **Вам с `газом?** [vʌm s `gʌzʌm]

1624. What kind of coffee have you got? - **Ка`кой у вас есть `кофе?** [kʌ`kɒj ʊ vʌs jest' `kɒf'e]

1625. I will take a / an ... - **Я `буду ...** [jʌ `bʊdʊ ...]

1626. ... Americano - **Амери`кано** [ʌm'er'i`kʌnʌ]

1627. ... Cocoa - **Ка`као** [kʌ`kʌɒ]

1628. ... Cappuccino - **Капу`чино** [kʌpʊ`tʃ'inʌ]

1629. ... Espresso - **Эсп`рессо** [esp`resʌ]

1630. ... Hot chocolate - **Го`рячий шоко`лад** [gʌ`r'ʌtʃ'ij ʃʌkʌ`lʌt]

1631. ... Latte - **`Латте** [`lʌte]

1632. Add sugar please - **Поло`жите, по`жалуйста, `сахар** [pʌlʌ`ʒit'e pʌ`ʒʌlʊstʌ `sʌhʌr]

1633. Without sugar, please - Без `сахара, по`жалуйста [b′es `sʌhʌrʌ pʌ`ʒʌlʊstʌ]

1634. With milk please - С моло`ком, по`жалуйста [s mʌlʌ`kɒm pʌ`ʒʌlʊstʌ]

1635. In a cup or in a teapot? - В `чашке `или в `чайнике? [v `tʃʌʃk′e `il′ɪ v `tʃʌjn′ik′e]

1636. A bottle or a glass? - Бу`тылку или бо`кал? [bʊ`tylkʊ `il′ɪ bʌ`kʌl]

1637. What kind of alcoholic drinks have you got? - Ка`кие у вас есть алко`гольные на`питки? [kʌ`k′ie ʊ vʌs jest′ ʌlkʌ`gɒl′nyje nʌ`p′itk′i]

1638. We have got ... - У нас есть ... [ʊ nʌs jest′ ...]

1639. ... Beer - `Пиво [`p′ivʌ]

1640. ... Brandy - Б`ренди [b`rend′i]

1641. ... Champagne - Шам`панское [ʃʌm`pʌnskʌje]

1642. ... Cider - Сидр [s′idr]

1643. ... Cognac - Конь`як [kʌn″jʌk]

1644. ... Gin - Джин [dʒin]

1645. ... Rum - Ром [rɒm]

1646. ... Tequila - Те`кила [te`k′ilʌ]

1647. ... Vodka - `Водка [`vɒtkʌ]

1648. ... Whisky - `Виски [`v′isk′i]

1649. ... (Red/White) Wine - (К`расное /`Белое) Ви`но [(k`rʌsnʌje / `b′elʌje) v′i`nɒ]

8.3. Post, Mobile and Internet Service

1650. I would like to send a letter / a parcel - Я хо`чу отп`равить пись`мо / по`сылку [jʌ hʌ`tʃʊ ʌtp`rʌv′it′ p′is″mɒ / pʌ`sylkʊ]

1651. I would like to buy a box for my parcel - **Я хо`чу ку`пить ко`робку для по`сылки** [jʌ hʌ`tʃu ku`p'it' kʌ`rɒpku dl'ʌ pʌ`sylk'i]

1652. I would like to buy stamps - **Я хо`чу ку`пить `марки** [jʌ hʌ`tʃu ku`p'it' `mʌrk'i]

1653. How long will the delivery take? - **С`колько зай`мёт пере`сылка?** [s`kɒl'kʌ zʌj`m'ɒt p'er'e`sylkʌ]

1654. Can I send ...? - **`Можно ли отправ`лять ...?** [`mɒʒnʌ l'ɪ ʌtprʌv`l'ʌt' ...]

1655. Do you want to send it by airmail? - **Вы хо`тите отп`равить авиа`почтой / эксп`ресс-`почтой?** [vy hʌ`t'it'e ʌtp`rʌv'it' ʌv'iʌ`pɒtʃtʌj / eksp`res `pɒtʃtʌj]

1656. I want to buy a postcard - **Я хо`чу ку`пить отк`рытку** [jʌ hʌ`tʃu ku`p'it' ʌtk`rytku]

1657. What is the track number for this parcel? - **Ка`кой `номер отс`леживания для `этой по`сылки?** [kʌ`kɒj `nɒm'er ʌts`l'eʒivʌn'ijʌ dl'ʌ `etʌj pʌ`sylk'i]

1658. I need to make a copy - **Мне `нужно с`делать `копию** [mn'e `nuʒnʌ s`d'elʌt' `kɒp'iju]

1659. I would like to print out some documents - **Мне `нужно распе`чатать доку`менты** [mn'e `nuʒnʌ rʌsp'e`tʃʌtʌt' dʌku`m'enty]

1660. I would like to buy a SIM card - **Я хо`чу ку`пить сим-`карту** [jʌ hʌ`tʃu ku`p'it' s'im`kʌrtu]

1661. Can I get a SIM card without Russian citizenship? - **`Можно ли полу`чить сим-`карту без рос`сийского граж`данства?** [`mɒʒnʌ l'i pʌlu`tʃ'it' s'im`kʌrtu b'es rʌ`s'ijskʌvʌ grʌʒ`dʌnstvʌ]

1662. I would like to have an Internet pack - **Я хо`чу подклю`чить па`кет интер`нета** [jʌ hʌ`tʃu pʌdklu`tʃ'it' pʌ`k'et inter`netʌ]

1663. How can I check my balance? – **Как уз`нать свой ба`ланс?** [kʌk ʊz`nʌt' svɒj bʌ`lʌns]

1664. How can I pay for the services? – **Как по`полнить ба`ланс?** [kʌk pʌ`pɒln'it' bʌ`lʌns]

1665. Are there any places with free Wi-Fi? – **Здесь есть мес`та с бесп`латным вай-`фаем?** [zd'es' jest' m'es`tʌ s b'esp`lʌtnym vʌj`fʌjem]

1666. Can you share Wi-Fi from your phone? – **Вы `можете раз`дать вай-фай с теле`фона?** [vy `mɒʒet'e rʌz`dʌt' vʌj`fʌj s t'el'e`fɒnʌ]

Chapter 9. Health and Safety

9.1. Medical Conditions and Emergencies

1667. I have medical insurance - **У ме`ня есть меди`цинская стра`ховка** [ʊ mʼeˋnʌ jestʼ mʼedʼiˋtsʼinskʌjʌ strʌˋhɒfkʌ]

1668. I have no medical insurance - **У ме`ня нет меди`цинской стра`ховки** [ʊ mʼeˋnʌ nʼet mʼedʼiˋtsʼinskʌj strʌˋhɒfkʼi]

1669. I need an ambulance - **Мне нуж`на с`корая `помощь** [mnʼe nʊʒˋnʌ sˋkɒrʌjʌ ˋpɒmʌʃʼ]

1670. Can you apply first aid? - **Вы `можете ока`зать `первую `помощь?** [vy ˋmɒʒetʼe ʌkʌˋzʌtʼ pʼervʊjʊ ˋpɒmʌʃʼ]

1671. I can apply first aid - **Я мо`гу ока`зать `первую `помощь** [jʌ mʌˋgʊ ʌkʌˋzʌtʼ pʼervʊjʊ ˋpɒmʌʃʼ]

1672. How can I call an ambulance? - **Как `вызвать с`корую?** [kʌk ˋvyzvʌtʼ sˋkɒrʊjʊ]

1673. Call an ambulance - **`Вызовите с`корую** [ˋvyzʌvʼitʼe sˋkɒrʊjʊ]

1674. Where is the nearest first-aid station? - **Где на`ходится бли`жайший травм`пункт?** [gdʼe nʌˋhɒdʼitsʌ blʼiˋʒʌjʃyj trʌvmˋpʊnkt]

1675. I need a ... - **Мне `нужен ...** [mnʼe ˋnʊʒen ...]

1676. ... Cardiologist - **Карди`олог** [kʌrdʼiˋɒlʌk]

1677. ... Dentist - **Зуб`ной врач** [zʊbˋnɒj vrʌtʃ]

1678. ... Dermatologist - **Дерма´толог** [dʼermʌˋtɒlʌk]

1679. ... GP - **Тера`певт** [terʌˋpʼeft]

1680. ... Gynecologist - **Гине`колог** [gʼinʼeˋkɒlʌk]

1681. ... Neurologist - **Невропа`толог** [nˈevrʌpʌ`tɒlʌk]

1682. ... Ophthalmologist - **Офталь`молог** [ʌftʌlʼ`mɒlʌk]

1683. ... Pediatrician - **Педи`атр** [pˈedʼi`ʌtr]

1684. ... Surgeon - **Хи`рург** [hˈi`rʊrk]

1685. ... Urologist - **У`ролог** [ʊ`rɒlʌk]

1686. I have got a chronic disease - **У ме`ня хро`ническая бо`лезнь** [ʊ mʼe`nʼʌ hrʌ`nʼitʃˈeskʌjʌ bʌ`lʼeznʼ]

1687. I feel bad - **Мне п`лохо** [mnʼe p`lɒhʌ]

1688. I'm aching all over - **У ме`ня всё бо`лит** [ʊ mʼe`nʼʌ fsʼɒ bʌ`lʼit]

1689. I feel dizzy - **У ме`ня к`ружится голо`ва** [ʊ mʼe`nʼʌ k`rʊʒʼitsʌ gʌlʌ`vʌ]

1690. I feel sick - **Ме`ня тош`нит** [mʼe`nʼʌ tʌʃ`nʼit]

1691. I passed out - **Я у`пал** (masculine) / **у`пала** (feminine) **в `обморок** [jʌ ʊ`pʌl / ʊ`pʌlʌ v `ɒbmʌrʌk]

1692. I have (a/an) ... - **У ме`ня ...** [ʊ mʼe`nʼʌ ...]

1693. ... (High/Low) Blood pressure - **(Вы`сокое / `Низкое) Дав`ление** [(vy`sɒkʌje / `nʼiskʌje) dʌv`lʼenʼije]

1694. ... Burnt - **О`жог** [ʌ`ʒɒk]

1695. ... Chill - **Оз`ноб** [ʌz`nɒp]

1696. ... Cough - **`Кашель** [`kʌʃelʼ]

1697. ... Cramps - **`Судороги** [`sʊdʌrʌgʼi]

1698. ... Diarrhea - **По`нос** [pʌ`nɒs]

1699. ... Dislocation - **`Вывих** [`vyvʼih]

1700. ... Fever - **Лихо`радка** [lʼihʌ`rʌtkʌ]

1701. ... Inflammation - **Воспа`ление** [vʌspʌ`l'en'ije]

1702. ... Indigestion - **Расст`ройство же`лудка** [rʌst`rɒjstvʌ ʒe`lʊtkʌ]

1703. ... Muscle ache - **Боль в `мышцах** [bɒl' v `myʃtsʌh]

1704. ... Rash - **Сыпь** [syp']

1705. ... Running nose - **`Насморк** [`nʌsmʌrk]

1706. ... Sprain - **Растя`жение** [rʌst'ʌ`ʒen'ije]

1707. ... Swelling - **При`пухлость** [pr'i`pʊhlʌst']

1708. ... Weakness - **С`лабость** [s`lʌbʌst']

1709. My ... is aching - **У ме`ня бо`лит ...** [ʊ m'e`n'ʌ bʌ`l'it ...]

1710. ... (Right/Left) Arm - **(П`равая/`Левая) Рука** [(p`rʌvʌjʌ/ `le'vʌjʌ) rʊ`kʌ]

(Note that there is one general word **ру`ка** in Russian, which means both an arm and a hand.)

1711. ... (Right/Left) Ankle - **(П`равая/`Левая) Ло`дыжка** [(p`rʌvʌjʌ/ `le'vʌjʌ) lʌ`dyʃkʌ]

1712. ... Back - **Спи`на** [sp'i`nʌ]

1713. ... Backbone - **Позво`ночник** [pʌzvʌ`nɒtʃn'ik]

1714. ... Belly - **Жи`вот** [ʒ'i`vɒt]

1715. ... Chest - **Грудь** [grʊt´]

1716. ... (Right/Left) Ear - **(П`равое/`Левое) `Ухо** [(p`rʌvʌje/ `le'vʌje) `ʊhʌ]

1717. ... (Right/Left) Eye - **(П`равый/`Левый) Глаз** [(p`rʌvyj/ `le'vyj) glʌs]

1718. ... Finger - **`Палец** [`pʌl'ets]

1719. ... (Right/Left) Foot - **(П`равая/`Левая) Ступ`ня** [(p`rʌvʌjʌ/ `le'vʌjʌ) stʊp`n'ʌ]

1720. ... Forearm - **Предп`лечье** [pr'etp`l'etʃ'je]

1721. ... Head - **Голо`ва** [gʌlʌ`vʌ]

1722. ... Heart - **`Сердце** [`s'ertse]

1723. ... (Right/Left) Knee - **(П`равое/`Левое) Ко`лено** [(p`rʌvʌje / `le'vʌje) kʌ`l'enʌ]

1724. ... (Right/Left) Leg - **(П`равая/`Левая) Но`га** [(p`rʌvʌjʌ/ `le'vʌjʌ) nʌ`gʌ]

1725. ... Lip - **Гу`ба** [gʊ`bʌ]

1726. ... Kidneys - **`Почки** [`pɒtʃk'i]

1727. ... Liver - **`Печень** [`p'etʃ'en']

1728. ... Lungs - **`Лёгкие** [`l'ɒhk'ije]

1729. ... Neck - **`Шея** [ʃejʌ]

1730. ... Nose - **Нос** [nɒs]

1731. ... Rib - **Реб`ро** [r'eb`rɒ]

1732. ... (Right/Left) Shoulder - **(П`равое/`Левое) Пле`чо** [(p`rʌvʌje/ `le'vʌje) pl'e`tʃɒ]

1733. ... Stomach - **Же`лудок** [ʒe`lʊdʌk]

1734. ... Throat - **`Горло** [`gɒrlʌ]

1735. ... Toe - **`Палец на но`ге** [`pʌl'ets nʌ nʌ`g'e]

1736. ... Teeth/Tooth - **Зуб / `Зубы** [zʊp / `zʊby]

1737. ... (Right/Left) Wrist - **(П`равое/`Левое) За`пястье** [(p`rʌvʌje/ `le'vʌje) zʌ`p'ʌst'je]

1738. I have cut my ...- **Я по`резал** (masculine) / **по`резала** (feminine) ... [jʌ pʌ`r'ezʌl / pʌ`r'ezʌlʌ ...]

1739. I have an injury - **У ме`ня т`равма** [ʊ m'e`n'ʌ t`rʌvmʌ]

1740. I am bleeding – **У ме`ня и`дёт кровь** [u m'e`n'ʌ i`d'ɒt krɒf']

1741. Do you take any medicine? – **Вы прини`маете ка`кие-нибудь ле`карства?** [vy pr'in'i`mʌjet'e kʌ`k'ien'ibut' l'e`kʌrstvʌ]

1742. I take ... – **Я прини`маю ...** [jʌ pr'in'i`mʌju ...]

1743. Where does it hurt? – **Где бо`лит?** [gd'e bʌ`l'it]

1744. It hurts! – **`Больно!** [`bɒl'nʌ]

1745. I have no allergy to any medicine – **У ме`ня нет аллер`гии на меди`цинские препа`раты** [u m'e`n'ʌ n'et ʌl'er`g'ii nʌ m'ed'i`ts'insk'ije pr'epʌ`rʌty]

1746. I have an allergy to ... – **У ме`ня аллер`гия на ...** [u m'e`n'ʌ ʌl'er`g'ijʌ nʌ ...]

1747. I have been hit by a car – **Ме`ня с`била ма`шина** [m'e`n'ʌ z`b'ilʌ mʌ`ʃinʌ]

1748. I have fallen – **Я у`пал** (masculine) / **у`пала** (feminine) [jʌ u`pʌl / u`pʌlʌ]

1749. How long have you had it? – **С`колько `это продол`жается?** [s`kɒl'kʌ `etʌ prʌdʌl`ʒʌjetsʌ]

1750. I have had it for ... days – **У ме`ня `это у`же ...** [u m'e`n'ʌ `etʌ u`ʒe ...]

   – After any numeral ending with 1 – except 11 – **день** [den']

   – After any numeral ending with 2, 3, 4 – except 12, 13, 14 – **дня** [dn´ʌ]

   – After the numerals 11-14 or any numeral ending with 0, 5, 6, 7, 8, 9 – **дней** [dn´ej]

See Numerals

1751. Do you feel the pain while touching it? – **`Больно, ког`да т`рогаю?** [`bɒl'nʌ kʌg`dʌ t`rɒgʌju]

1752. Open your mouth please - Отк`ройте рот [ʌtk`rɒjt'e rɒt]

1753. Breathe / Do not breathe - Ды`шите / Не ды`шите [dy`ʃyt'e / n'e dy`ʃyt'e]

1754. What have you eaten / drunk in the last 24 hours? - Что вы `ели / `пили за пос`ледние `сутки? [ʃtɒ vy `jel'i / `p'il'i zʌ pʌs`l'edn'ije `sʊtk'i]

1755. I feel pain when I ... - Мне `больно, ког`да я ... [mn'e `bɒl'nʌ kʌg`dʌ jʌ ...]

1756. ... Eat - Ем [jem]

1757. ... Lie - Ле`жу [l'e`ʒʊ]

1758. ... Move - Д`вигаюсь [d`v'igʌjʊs']

1759. ... Sit - Си`жу [s'i`ʒʊ]

1760. ... Swallow - Гло`таю [glʌ`tʌjʊ]

1761. ... Walk - Хо`жу [hʌ`ʒʊ]

1762. I feel nothing - Я ниче`го не `чувствую [jʌ n'itʃe`vɒ n'e `tʃʊvstvʊjʊ]

1763. You need to have a blood test - `Нужно сдать а`нализ к`рови [`nʊʒnʌ zdʌt' ʌ`nʌl'iz `krɒv'i]

1764. You need some stitches - `Нужно нало`жить швы [`nʊʒnʌ nʌlʌ`ʒ'it' ʃvy]

1765. You need an X-ray / ultrasound - `Нужно сделать рент`ген / ультраз`вук [`nʊʒnʌ z`d'elʌt' r'en`g'en / ʊl'trʌz`vʊk]

1766. Do I need an operation? - Мне нуж`на опе`рация? [mn'e `nʊʒnʌ ʌp'e`rʌts'ijʌ]

1767. I will prescribe you some medicine - Я `выпишу вам ле`карство [jʌ `vyp'iʃʊ vʌm l'e`kʌrstvʌ]

1768. You will have to stay in the hospital – **Вам при`дётся ос`таться в боль`нице** [vʌm pr'i`d'ɒtsʌ ʌs`tʌt'sʌ v bʌl'`n'itse]

1769. I will give you an injection – **Я с`делаю вам у`кол** [jʌ z`d'elʌju vʌm u`kɒl]

1770. I will put on a plaster – **Я нало`жу гипс** [jʌ nʌlʌ`ʒu g'ips]

1771. I will dress the wound – **Я перевя`жу `рану** [ʌ p'er'ev'ʌ`ʒu `rʌnu]

1772. I feel better now – **Мне `лучше** [mn'e `lutʃe]

9.2. Emergency Situations

1773. Call the emergency services! – **Зво`ните сто две`надцать!** [zvʌ`n'it'e stɒ dv'e`nʌtsʌt']

(Note that **сто двенадцать – 112 –** is the Russian telephone number for emergency situations.)

1774. How can I call the police? – **Как `вызвать по`лицию?** [kʌk `vyzvʌt' pʌ`l'itsiju]

1775. Help! – **Помо`гите!** [pʌmʌ`g'it'e]

1776. Call the police – **`Вызовите по`лицию** [`vyzʌv'it'e pʌ`l'itsiju]

1777. I have had my ... stolen – **У ме`ня ук`рали ...** [u m'e`n'ʌ uk`rʌl'i ...]

1778. ... Bag – **`Сумку** [`sumku]

1779. ... Baggage – **Ба`гаж** [bʌ`gʌʒ]

1780. ... Car – **Ма`шину** [mʌ`ʃinu]

1781. ... Documents – **Доку`менты** [dʌku`m'enty]

1782. ... Money – **`Деньги** [`d'en'g'i]

1783. ... Wallet – **Коше`лёк** [kʌʃe`l'ɒk]

1784. There is a fight - Здесь д`рака [zd'es' d`rʌkʌ]

1785. I have been attacked - На ме`ня на`пали [nʌ m'e`n'ʌ nʌ`pʌl'i]

1786. I have been robbed - Ме`ня ог`рабили [m'e`n'ʌ ʌg`rʌb'il'i]

1787. I am being robbed - Ме`ня пы`таются ог`рабить [m'e`n'ʌ py`tʌjutsʌ ʌg`rʌb'it']

1788. I have been raped - Ме`ня изна`силовали [m'e`n'ʌ iznʌ`s'ilʌvʌl'i]

1789. I am being raped - Ме`ня пы`таются изна`силовать [m'e`n'ʌ py`tʌjutsʌ iznʌ`s'ilʌvʌt']

1790. I have got lost - Я заблу`дился (masculine) / заблу`дилась (feminine) [jʌ zʌblu`d'ils'ʌ / zʌblu`d'ilʌs']

1791. Call the fire brigade! - Вызы`вайте по`жарных! [vyzy`vʌjt'e pʌ`ʒʌrnyh]

1792. My car is burning! - Мо`я ма`шина го`рит! [mʌ`jʌ mʌ`ʃinʌ gʌ`r'it]

1793. Fire! - По`жар! [pʌ`ʒʌr]

1794. Leave the building! - По`кинуть з`дание! [pʌ`k'iymut z`dʌn'ije]

1795. It smells like gas - Я `чувствую `запах `газа [jʌ `tʃuvstvuju `zʌpʌh `gʌzʌ]

1796. There has been an accident - Произош`ла а`вария [prʌ'izʌ`ʃlʌ ʌ`vʌr'ijʌ]

1797. Someone is sinking - Чело`век `тонет [tʃ'elʌ`v'ek `tɒn'et]

1798. There has been an explosion - Произо`шёл взрыв [prʌ'izʌ`ʃ'ɒl vz`ryf]

1799. My address is ... - Мой `адрес ... [mɒj `ʌdr'es ...]

1800. I am a foreigner - **Я иност`ранец** (masculine) / **иност`ранка** (feminine) [jʌ inʌst`rʌn'ets / inʌst`rʌnkʌ]

1801. I need to contact the ambassy - **Мне `нужно свя`заться с по`сольством** [mn'e `nuʒnʌ sv'ʌ`zʌtsʌ s pʌ`sɒl'stvʌm]

Chapter 10. Time and Measurements

10.1. Measurements

Note that there is the internationally recognized metric system used in Russia.

Thus, there are millimeters – **милли`метры** [m'il'i`m'etry], centimeters – **санти`метры** [sʌnt'i`m'etry], meters – **`метры** [`m'etry], and kilometers – **кило`метры** [k'ilʌ`m'etry] – used for distance measuring:

- After any numeral ending with 1 – except 11 – **милли`метр / санти`метр / метр / кило`метр** [m'il'i`m'etr / sʌnt'i`m'etr / m'etr / k'ilʌ`metr]

- After any numeral ending with 2, 3, 4 – except 12, 13, 14 – **милли`метра / санти`метра / `метра / кило`метра** [m'il'i`m'etrʌ / sʌnt'i`m'etrʌ / `m'etrʌ / k'ilʌ`metrʌ]

- After the numerals 11-14 or any numeral ending with 0, 5, 6, 7, 8, 9 – **милли`метров / санти`метров / `метров / кило`метров** [m'il'i`m'etrʌf / sʌnt'i`m'etrʌf / `m'etrʌf / k'ilʌ`metrʌf]

Grams – **г`раммы** [g`rʌmy] – and kilograms – **килог`раммы** [k'ilʌg`rʌmy] – are used for weight measuring:

- After any numeral ending with 1 – except 11 – **грамм / килог`рамм** [grʌm / k'ilʌg`rʌm]

- After any numeral ending with 2, 3, 4 – except 12, 13, 14 – **г`рамма / килог`рамма** [g`rʌmʌ / k'ilʌg`rʌmʌ]

- After the numerals 11-14 or any numeral ending with 0, 5, 6, 7, 8, 9 – **г`раммов / килог`раммов** [g`rʌmʌf / k'ilʌg`rʌmʌf]

Liters – **литры** [`l'itry] – are used for volume measuring:

- After any numeral ending with 1 – except 11 – **литр** [l'itr]

- After any numeral ending with 2, 3, 4 – except 12, 13, 14 – **литра** [`l'itrʌ]

- After the numerals 11-14 or any numeral ending with 0, 5, 6, 7, 8, 9 – **литров** [`l'itrʌf]

Square meters – **квадратные метры** [kvʌd`rʌtnyje `m'etry] – and square kilometers – **квадратные километры** [kvʌd`rʌtnyje k'ilʌ`m'etry] are used for surface measuring:

- After any numeral ending with 1 – except 11 – **квадратный метр / километр** [kvʌd`rʌtnyj `m'etr / k'ilʌ`m'etr]

- After any numeral ending with 2, 3, 4 – except 12, 13, 14 – **квадратных метра / километра** [kvʌd`rʌtnyh `m'etrʌ / k'ilʌ`m'etrʌ]

- After the numerals 11-14 or any numeral ending with 0, 5, 6, 7, 8, 9 – **квадратных метров / километров** [kvʌd`rʌtnyh `m'etrʌf / k'ilʌ`m'etrʌf]

To measure temperature, the Celsius scale is used, with degrees Celsius = ºC:

- After any numeral ending with 1 – except 11 – **г`радус** [g`rʌdʊs]

- After any numeral ending with 2, 3, 4 – except 12, 13, 14 – **г`радуса** [g`rʌdʊsʌ]

- After the numerals 11-14 or any numeral ending with 0, 5, 6, 7, 8, 9 – **г`радусов** [g`rʌdʊsʌf].

10.2. Time

1802. What is the time? – **С`колько в`ремени?** [s`kɒl'kʌ v`r'em'en'i]

(Note that both the 12-hour and 24-hour clocks are used in Russia. The latter is always used for schedules, official information, etc. We will not analyze the 12-hour clock here because it is quite complicated, and one needs to use various additional words. Here, we will use the 24-hour clock as it is much easier and is generally accepted across the country.)

1803. It is ... now – **Сей`час ...** [s´ej`tʃʌs ...]

To tell the time with the 24-hour clock system, you have to say first the hours and then the minutes – e.g. **22.00**. (Note that a dot will be used here rather that a colon – and the number will sound like: **д`вадцать два ноль-ноль** [d`vʌtsʌt' dvʌ nɒl'-nɒl'] – literally twenty two zero-zero; **15.30** will sound like: **пят`надцать т`ридцать** [p'ʌt`nʌtsʌt' tr'idtsʌt] – literally fifteen thirty, etc.)

See Numerals

1804. When – **Ког`да?** [kʌg`dʌ]

1805. Today – **Се`годня** [s'e`vɒdn'ʌ]

1806. Yesterday – **Вче`ра** [vtʃ'e`rʌ]

1807. The day before yesterday – **Позавче`ра** [pʌzʌv`tʃ'erʌ]

1808. Tomorrow – **`Завтра** [`zʌftrʌ]

1809. The day after tomorrow – **После`завтра** [pɒsl'e`zʌvtrʌ]

1810. Now – **Сей`час** [s´ej`tʃʌs]

1811. Not now – **Не сей`час** [n'e s´ej`tʃʌs]

1812. Then – **Тог`да** [tʌg`dʌ]

1813. A bit later – **По`позже** [pʌ`pɒʒe]

1814. Soon – **С`коро** [s`kɒrʌ]

1815. In ... seconds / minutes / hours / days – **`Через ...** [`tʃ'er'ez]

- After any numeral ending with 1 – except 11 – **се`кунду / ми`нуту / час/ день** [s´e`kʋndʋ / m'i`nʋtʋ / tʃʌs/ d'en']

- After any numeral ending with 2, 3, 4 – except 12, 13, 14 – **се`кунды / ми`нуты / ча`са/ дня** [s´e`kʋndy / m'i`nʋty / tʃʌ`sʌ/ dn'ʌ]

- After the numerals 11-14 or any numeral ending with 0, 5, 6, 7, 8, 9 – **се`кунд / ми`нут / ча`сов/ дней** [s´e`kʋnd / m'i`nʋt / tʃʌ`sɒf/ dn'ej]

1816. In the morning – **`Утром** [`ʋtrʌm]

1817. At midday – **В `полдень** [v `pɒld'en']

1818. In the afternoon – **Днём** [dn'ɒm]

1819. In the evening – **`Вечером** [`ʋ´etʃerʌm]

1820. At midnight – **В `полночь** [v `pɒlnʌtʃ']

1821. At night – **`Ночью** ['nɒtʃjʋ]

1822. It is late – **`Поздно** [`pɒznʌ]

1823. It is early – **`Рано** [`rʌnʌ]

1824. Never – **Никог`да** [n'ikʌg`dʌ]

1825. Often – **`Часто** [`tʃʌstʌ]

1826. Seldom – **`Редко** [`r'etkʌ]

1827. Always – **Всег`да** [fs'eg`dʌ]

1828. What day is it today? – **Ка`кой се`годня день?** [kʌ`kɒj s'e`vɒdn'ʌ d'en']

1829. ... Monday – **Поне`дельник** [pʌn'e`d'el'n'ik]

1830. ... Tuesday – **В`торник** [f`tɒrn'ik]

1831. ... Wednesday – **Сре`да** [sr'e`dʌ]

1832. ... Thursday – **Чет`верг** [tʃ´et`v´erk]

1833. ... Friday – **`Пятница** [`p´ʌtn'itsʌ]

1834. ... Saturday - **Суб`бота** [sʊ`bɒtʌ]

1835. ... Sunday - **Воскре`сенье** [vʌskr′e`s′en′je]

1836. What month is it now? - **Ка`кой сей`час `месяц?** [kʌ`kɒj s′ej`tʃʌs `m′esʌts]

1837. ... January - **Ян`варь** [jʌn`vʌr′]

1838. ... February - **Фев`раль** [f′ev`rʌl′]

1839. ... March - **Март** [mʌrt]

1840. ... April - **Ап`рель** [ʌp`r′el′]

1841. ... May - **Май** [mʌj]

1842. ... June - **И`юнь** [ɪ`jʊn′]

1843. ... July - **И`юль** [ɪ`jʊl′]

1844. ... August - **`Август** [`ʌvgʊst]

1845. ... September - **Се`нтябрь** [s′en`t′ʌbr′]

1846. ... October - **Ок`тябрь** [ʌk`t′ʌbr′]

1847. ... November - **Но`ябрь** [nʌ`jʌbr′]

1848. ... December - **Де`кабрь** [d′e`kʌbr′]

1849. What is being celebrated today? - **Что се`годня отме`чают?** [ʃtɒ s′e`vɒdn′ʌ ʌtm′e`tʃʌjʊt]

1850. New Year - **`Новый год** [`nɒvyj gɒt]

(Note that New Year is celebrated on December 31st and overnight into January 1st.)

1851. Christmas - **Рождест`во** [rʌʒd′est`vɒ]

(Note that most Russians celebrate the Orthodox Christmas - overnight from January 6th into January 7th.)

1852. Defender of the Fatherland Day - **День за`щитника О`течества** [d′en′ zʌ`ʃ′itn′ikʌ ʌ`t′etʃ′estvʌ]

(Note that this is an official public holiday, which is celebrated on February 23rd. It is usually perceived as a kind of men's day, when all male friends and relatives are congratulated, but there is also usually an official side to the celebration, with military parades etc.)

1853. International Women's Day – **Междуна`родный `женский `день** [m′eʒdʊnʌ`rɒdnyj `ʒensk′ij d′en′]

(Note that this day – March 8th – is also a public holiday, it is usually celebrated as a kind of women's day, when all female friends and relatives are congratulated.)

1854. Spring and Labour Day – **День вес`ны и тру`да** [d′en′ v′es`ny ɪ t`rʊdʌ]

(Note that this holiday takes place around May 1st, and it usually lasts for several days.)

1855. Victory Day – **День Победы** [d′en′ pʌ`b′edy]

(Note that the WWII Victory Day is celebrated on May 9th, it also usually involves several days-off.)

1856. Russia Day – **День Рос`сии** [d′en′ rʌ`s′ii]

(Note that this is usually celebrated on June 12th.)

1857. Unity Day – **День на`родного е`динства** [d′en′ nʌ`rɒdnʌvʌ je`d′instvʌ]

(Note that this former Soviet Revolution Day is celebrated for several days and takes place around November 4th.)

In addition to these official holidays, there are also many memorable dates that are celebrated in Russia without public holidays. The major ones include:

- Tatiana Day – **Тат`ьянин день** [tʌt″jʌn′in d′en′], which is celebrated on January 25th as a kind of Student Day.

- St Valentine's Day – **День свя`того Вален`тина** [dˊen' svʼʌ`tɒvʌ vʌlʼen`tʼinʌ] on February 14th.

- Maslenitsa – **`Масленица** [`mʌslʼenʼitsʌ], which is a traditional Slavic celebration that takes place during the week before Great Lent; the dates change every year, depending on the beginning of Great Lent. This celebration involves various traditions, e.g. eating traditional Russian pancakes – **бли`ны** [blʼi`ny].

- Cosmonautics Day – **День космо`навтики** [dˊen' kʌsmʌ`nʌftʼikʼi], which is celebrated on April 12th and commemorates the first manned space flight.

- Easter – **`Пасха** [`pʌshʌ], which is celebrated according to the Orthodox calendar but does not involve any public holidays.

- Knowledge Day – **День з`наний** [dˊen' z`nʌnʼij], which is celebrated on September 1st and marks the beginning of a school year for both school pupils and university students.

Index

A

Accessories – 7.3

Accommodation – 8.1

Age – 4.1

Alcohol – 8.2

Alphabet – 1.1

Airport – 5.1

ATM – 7.1

B

Body Parts – 9.1
Books – 7.4
Bus – 5.4

C

Car rent – 5.5
Cardinal Numerals – 2.1
Cinema – 6.1
Clothes – 7.3
Collecting – 4.4
Colours – 7.3
Conjugation – 1.2
Cosmetics – 7.6
Countries – 5.1
Cuisine – 8.2
Currency Exchange – 7.1
Customs – 5.1

D

Dairy Products – 8.2
Days of the Week – 10.2
Desserts – 8.2
Diseases – 9.1
Distance – 10.1
Doctors – 9.1
Documents – 3.4
Drinks – 8.2

E

Electronics – 7.5

Emergency Situations – 9.2

F

Fabric Prints – 7.3

Fabrics – 7.3

Family – 4.2

Films – 6.1

Finances – 7.1

Fish – 8.2

Flowers – 7.4

Food – 8.2

Fruit – 8.2

G

Gemstones – 7.3

Gender Aspect – 1.2

General Expressions – 3.1

Getting Around – 5.2

Grains – 8.2

Grammar Principles in Russian – 1.2

Grammatical Cases – 1.2

Greetings – 3.1

H

Hobbies – 4.4

Honorific Forms – 1.2

Hospital – 9.1

Hostels – 8.1

Hotels – 8.1

Householdware – 7.5

I

Interests – 4.4

Internet – 8.1, 8.3

Introducing – 4.1

J

Jobs – 4.3

L

Language – 3.2

M

Materials – 7.3

Medicine – 7.6

Measurements – 10.1

Meat – 8.2

Medical Conditions – 7.6, 9.1

Metals – 7.3

Minor Ailments – 7.6

Mobile Service – 8.3

Money – 7.1

Months – 10.2

Museum – 6.2

Musical Instruments – 4.4

N

Nationalities – 4.1

Nightlife – 6.1

Numerals – 2.1, 2.2

Nuts – 8.1

O

On board of a plane – 5.1

Ordinal Numerals – 2.2

P

Passport Control – 5.1

Personal Hygiene Products – 7.6

Personal Pronouns – 1.2

Phone Conversations – 3.3

Post – 8.3

Professions – 4.3

Pronunciation Rules – 1.1

Public Holidays – 10.2

R

Reading Rules – 1.1

Relationships – 4.2

Renting a Flat – 8.1

Restaurant – 8.2

S

Seafood – 8.2

Security Screening – 5.1

Shoes – 7.3

Shopping – 7.2, 7.3, 7.4, 7.5, 7.6

Shops – 7.1

Sightseeing – 6.1

Sizes – 7.3

Sport – 4.4

Stationery – 7.4

Subway – 5.4

Surface – 10.1

T

Taxi – 5.5

Temperature – 10.1

Theater – 6.1, 6.2

Tickets – 5.3, 5.4, 6.1, 6.2

Time – 10.2

Trains – 5.3

Tram – 5.4

Trolleybus – 5.4

V

Volume – 10.1

Vegetables – 8.2

W

Weight – 10.1

Word Order – 1.2

Check out another book by Simple Language Learning

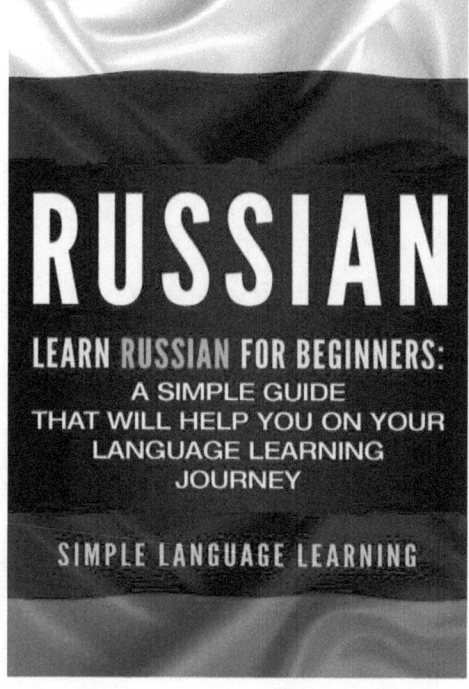

www.ingramcontent.com/pod-product-compliance
Lightning Source LLC
Chambersburg PA
CBHW030114100526
44591CB00009B/400